TRAVELS WITH JOE

TRAVELS WITH JOE

1917-1993

THE LIFE STORY OF A HISTORIAN FROM TEXAS

BY DAVID G. MCCOMB

TEXAS STATE HISTORICAL ASSOCIATION

AUSTIN

FOR ALL OF THOSE WHO LOVED HIM

Library of Congress Cataloging-in-Publication Data
McComb, David G.
    Travels with Joe: the life story of a historian from Texas, 1917–1993/ by David G. McComb.
        p. cm.
    Includes bibliographical references and index.
    ISBN 0-87611-181-9 (alk. paper)
    1. Frantz, Joe Bertram, 1917-1993. 2. Historians--United States--Biography. 3. Historians--Texas--Biography. 4. Texas--Biography. I. Title.
        E175.5 .F77 2001
        973'.07'202--dc21
        [B]   00-053647

    10 9 8 7 6 5 4 3 2 1

Published by the Texas State Historical Association in Cooperation with the Center for Studies in Texas History at the University of Texas at Austin.

Book design by Janice Pinney.

The paper used in this book meets the minimum requirements of the American National Standard for Permanence of Paper for Printed Library Materials, Z39.48-1984.

This book was made possible in part by a grant from the Frantz History Enhancement Fund, College of Arts and Humanities, Texas A&M University-Corpus Christi.

CONTENTS

PROLOGUE

His journey came to an end on a mixed day of clouds and sunshine, November 13, 1993. Local newspapers and the *New York Times* printed brief obituaries of this western historian and, three days later, in its section "Across the USA: News From Every State," *USA Today* noted succinctly, "A memorial service is Saturday for Joe B. Frantz, 76, a close friend of Lyndon B. Johnson and the unofficial curator of the LBJ Presidential library, who died of complications from diabetes Saturday."

There had been a month of declining health and confusion of mind in Hermann Hospital in Houston; his only options were heart surgery and continual dialysis for the kidney failure caused by diabetes. He did not know what city he was in, nor could he supply the other simple pieces of information interns always ask for in determining the mental condition of their patients. Near the end he was unable to name the president of the United States—but said with a lingering flash of wit about the Republican minority leader of the Senate, "Bob Dole thinks he is!"[1]

Death, as we all know but do not like to contemplate, can be messy and unpleasant and prolonged. Thoughtfully, based upon family experience, Joe B. Frantz wrote in his will in 1991:

I do not wish to be continued one minute beyond my usefulness. I have lived three-quarters of a century doing pretty much as I pleased, helping others while helping myself. I have pride and dignity, and I am horrified by the prospect of attaining a dependent stage. I may have made a mess of some portions of my life, but it was my mess, and usually I enjoyed making it. When I can no longer actively bring service, pleasure, and love to the world around me, cancel me QUICKLY. This is not a request; it is a fervent order meant to be carried out quietly, and efficiently. And no one is to look back![2]

Friends from Corpus Christi visited the dying professor in the hospital, and as he phased into a coma Betsy Chadderdon Frantz, his fourth wife, invited his first family to come see him. Helen B. Frantz and his adult daughters Jolie and Lisa were with him when he passed away. In the terse manner of physicians the death certificate noted pneumonia and multiorgan failure as the cause of dying.[3] The body was cremated, and a place reserved for him in the State Cemetery of Texas by orders of Governor Ann W. Richards. He would reside in Valhalla with the heroes of Texas and the giants of Southwestern literature, J. Frank Dobie and Walter Prescott Webb.[4]

There were memorial services in both Corpus Christi and Austin, places where he had made the greatest impact. In Corpus Christi at the Texas A&M-Corpus Christi Center for the Arts, John Owings played a piano piece composed by Lawrence Weiner, "Remembrance—in Memory of Joe B. Frantz." Frantz's colleagues reminisced with a rare homemade video of him and a close friend, Jim McClellan, musing about their lives and activities.[5] In Austin at the Bass Lecture Hall of the Lyndon Baines Johnson Library, with "Cactus" Pryor, a local journalist and radio commentator, acting as master of ceremonies, various speakers recounted Frantz's generosity, love of music, and insatiable interest in travel. The service began with a jazz recording by Oscar Peterson and ended with Frank Sinatra singing "Oh, the Good Life," music assembled by his stepdaughter, Liz Chadderdon. Ricardo Romo, a scholar and now president of the University of Texas at San Antonio, told the crowded room about Frantz's friendship and encouragement. Writer Don Graham characterized Frantz as a historian who managed to live in the present, and Luci Baines Johnson related how the professor had buoyed her spirits at a time of despair by making her feel worthy, bright, dignified, and hopeful.

Michael Gillette, a former student and later colleague in oral history work, said Frantz was an "institution," and an "Austin original." "He moved gracefully in sophisticated circles of academia and politics. He was always at ease with ordinary people . . . he was brilliant but never pedantic, always timely but seldom punctual, civilized but hardly conventional. He was the most uncommon commoner I have ever known." Gillette tearfully and haltingly characterized the many adventures with Joe that he and others had experienced, "It was not the event or the destination of these trips that mattered," he said, "but it was the journey itself in his special company."[6]

So it was.

BEGINNINGS

Nearly everyone looked upon Joe B. Frantz as a personal friend. For most people, he was simply "Joe," not "Doctor," or "Professor." For some he was "Joe B." For those of us, subordinate and young, who worked with him on the LBJ Oral History Project he was "Chief," or the Spanish equivalent, "El Jefe." We were too reticent to call him "Joe," but he seemed to like his new title. He explained his feelings about all of this in a letter to "Wilbur:"

> Oh yes, I have never cared for titles, so if you could quietly drop the "Dr." before my name, I would feel better. I dropped any feeling I had for titles when I was a graduate student when I read that the Turks, who had little use for women as equal citizens, would not award them the same honors they gave men. Lord Halifax was the ambassador there just before World War II, and his wife was extremely active in charitable work. The Turks wanted to honor her, so they had a big ceremony and presented her with a medal and a ribbon that said "ORDER OF CHASTITY—2nd CLASS!"[1]

He preferred this familiarity, did not mind the interruption of friends, and wished to avoid the disease of arrogance that often infected academic people. Once, while he was chairman of the history department at the University of Texas, a well-known western historian, Wayne Gard, wrote and asked him to lunch. An unwitting assistant writing for Frantz told Gard he had to make an appointment. On the file copy of the reply Frantz angrily scribbled, "No more of this sort of thing—I always will find time for my friends. This makes me sound like I'm full of self esteem!" When Frantz was director of the Texas State Historical Association, a longtime secretary commented, "I must have heard a thousand times various unannounced visitors say, 'I was just passing by on the Interstate and dropped in to say hello. . . .'"[2]

Frantz had an expansive capacity for friendship unbounded by class or race. A mail clerk at the Texas State Historical Association, for instance, bounced into the office one day and announced with pleasure that the director had noticed him on the streets of Austin and stopped to talk. The young man was amazed at the attention he had received from a famous man. For another example, Frantz gave a eulogy for a former black maid, Ara Sheffield, whom he admired for her determination and grit. While the fires for integration raged she had told him how a white lady complained that the result would be that ". . . all the Negroes will want to come have tea with me, and sit on my front porch and visit." Ara Sheffield retorted, "I told her that some blacks may come to sit on your front porch, but I won't. I've got better things to do." Sheffield never returned to work for that white lady.[3]

She also refused to ride the bus the four miles from east to west Austin for house cleaning, so Frantz had to give her a lift. She slyly insisted on this so that she could question him about the current events of the day, and she chided him when he did not know the answers. It was her form of self-education. "I felt that somehow even my best wasn't exactly good enough for Ara," Frantz said in the eulogy, "for I knew that she never gave less than her best. . . . Over and over I found myself trying to live up to her principles, and am undoubtedly a better person because of her."[4]

His immeasurable interest in human beings was genuine, but underneath it there existed his own need to be accepted and admired. According to psychologist Abraham Maslow and his hierarchy of needs, everyone needs acceptance. In Frantz, however there was an insatiable thirst that can be traced to his very early childhood, and involves a remarkable story. His birth certificate issued from Dallas states that Joe Bertram Frantz was born on January 16, 1917, and that his father Ezra Allen Frantz and his mother Mary Lavana Buckley were both from Weatherford, Texas.[5] According to family information, however, there is much more. Joe was adopted, not just once, but twice. His biological parents in Dallas died of influenza, probably part of the Spanish flu pandemic of 1917–1918, and a grandmother tried to care for the baby. It was too much and she placed the child in an orphanage. A couple named Marable adopted the baby, but the mother developed a brain tumor and the father left home. The child again went to an orphanage.

It is unclear how the young boy arrived at the shelter in Fort Worth, but it may have been according to a pattern of the time and place. In 1897 a Methodist minister, Reverend Isaac Z. T. Morris established the Texas Children's Home and Aid Society to take charge of abandoned children placed on westward-bound trains. At stations, workers placed the children with their name tags up on the top of crates—hence the expression "up for adoption." Morris met these orphan trains in Fort Worth, cared for the children and tried to match them with adoptive parents. Edna Gladney from Sherman began to work in the home in 1924 and took over fully when Morris retired the following year. In her honor, the home became the Gladney Center in 1950.[6]

Meanwhile, Mary "Mamie" Buckley Frantz of Weatherford, a small town forty miles west of Fort Worth, asked a woman in the larger town to watch for a baby boy who looked like the family. Her husband, Ezra, was reluctant to add a fifth child, but, when notified, he was willing to go to Morris's orphanage to look. Perhaps there might be a "Joe" to name after his stepfather. There on May 28, 1918, the sixteen-month-old boy toddled over to Ezra, grasped his leg, climbed in his lap, and held on. Ezra cuddled the blue-eyed child, stood up, and said, "Mamie, please fill out the papers. Little Joe and I are going outside."[7]

Joe always knew that he had been adopted—this was never a secret in the family—but he never found out much about his background. Could a child of that age be influenced by the experience of the orphanages? Psychologists would answer yes. To be given up for adoption is a rejection, incomprehensible for a helpless child who is trying to establish a secure bond with an adult. In this case, it was a double rejection, which might well explain Joe's unusual desire for acceptance and friendship. One of the earliest manifestations of this desire to please, Mary Frantz later told him, was a reluctance to touch the edge of a table, as if he had been scolded when trying to learn to walk.[8] Seemingly, this very early background affected Joe for the rest of his life.

There were four other children in the Frantz family—Ray, Ruby, Nellie, and Josephine. They were all older, with Ray already twenty years old when Joe entered the family. Ray was largely gone, on his way to an English Ph.D. and a teaching career at the University of Nebraska. He may well have provided for his little brother, nonetheless, an example of how education can lead to a world larger than Weatherford. Ruby, the second in line, was more of a curiosity for young Joe. She remained at home, married late, and vainly refused eyeglasses until the time came that she could no longer reach the piano pedals after pushing the bench back far enough to read the music. She sometimes mixed up words, such as once while serving coffee at night—"Oh, drink it! It's Sanka, has all the canine taken out of it." She and Ray died in 1976, ten days apart. Ruby had been in a rest home and Joe later reflected, "Why cloud the fine picture of a good life with the smudges and tarnish of a year or years in which we have no control of our faculties, but just lie there mindless."[9]

The Frantz home on Bridge Street. Joe B. Frantz's formative years were lived in Weatherford, Texas, where he developed a love of sports, music, and learning. *Photograph by David G. McComb.*

Nellie accompanied Little Joe, as he was called, to the first three days of the first grade, made him study when his marks faltered in the seventh grade, and gave him his first driving lessons.[10] He remained close to his family, at least until his break-up with Helen in 1978–1980. Joe was related to fifty-eight people in Weatherford and spent his formative years there, although the Frantz family lived in Fort Worth for six years, and in Florida for three years while his father tested the Florida land boom of the 1920s.

Ezra Frantz was an inventor, machinist, and businessman who in 1902 perfected a successful wire buckle for binding compressed cotton bales. He assembled the first automobile in Weatherford, but installed the gears incorrectly—so the car drove backwards. He came from Illinois and was a member of the fundamentalist Christian group, the Church of the Brethren. His harshest word was "Gentle-men!" Once, however, Joe heard him say, "Oh, Pshaw!"

after mashing his thumb with a hammer. "I felt as if I had been present at the Second Coming of the Devil," Little Joe thought.[11] The father's religion, however, did not rub off on the child—at the most, Joe became a sometime Methodist. Ezra, eighty-nine years old, died in 1964 after a time of senility. Joe observed and resolved, "I want to leave at full speed, not just wither away, a blank staring at a blank wall."[12]

Mary Buckley Frantz, afraid of strangers, foreigners, big cities, and sin, had grown up in Weatherford. She was stubborn, with little education, but though an uncle said reading would ruin Little Joe, she let the child read all he wished. She scolded her precocious son, however, when enticed by neighborhood kids he chalked dirty words on the sidewalk. She also forced him to use the word "Dear" in the salutation of a thank-you letter to a Sunday school girl who had given him a present. He had balked because he thought it obligated him to marry her.

Mamie would not eat at cafes that served wine, and on a visit to Los Angeles she refused to allow Joe out of the car to see the footprints of the stars in the cement because it was a "tourist place." She also refused him exit when they visited Calexico. Joe later concluded, "I think then was when I decided to spend as much time as possible traveling."[13] She died in 1951 and was remembered for her charity and for sending flowers to the funerals of little-known people, so that, as she said, "They will know someone in this world cares."[14]

Weatherford, the county seat of Parker County with a population of 6,203 in 1920, was located in dry, hilly country with stunted, medium-sized trees which foretold the arid prairie lands to the west. At 612 Bridge Street the Frantz family lived in a two-story house just five blocks from the city square. "The farmers would all come to town on Saturdays and the first Mondays with their loads of watermelons and the whole square would be clogged with wagons and with farmers around selling their watermelons," Joe recalled. "Kids squealing and little farm kids sitting on a block of salt and looking miserable and out of place, waiting for the time to go home, and women visiting with their aprons on."[15]

At Christmas time the family, holding nothing back, ate turkey, mashed potatoes, sweet potatoes, peas, biscuits, gravy, cornbread dressing, and six desserts including fudge divinity. Ruby, the eldest sister, was a notably good cook—and she always left something out when she shared recipes, according to Joe, so that no one else could match her. Little Joe was not neglected when it came to presents and he played with his baseballs in the coming months until they were just spheres of tight string held together with black friction tape.[16]

Joe acquired his love of sports in these years, particularly baseball and tennis. He broke the middle finger of his right hand at the first knuckle playing sandlot baseball. The Weatherford doctor thought it not worth fixing, and as a result Frantz lost full extension of the finger at the top. "I have no after effects although it makes 'showing the finger' to foes a mite more spectacular," he later quipped.[17] He was small-boned and not very big. He weighed 44 pounds at age eight, 80 pounds at age thirteen, 105 pounds in high school, and 125 at the time of marriage.[18] He eventually achieved a height of five feet, nine inches and put on additional poundage during his early professorial years. He developed a double chin, the kind some call a turkey-gobbler chin, and was described by a Washington, D.C., journalist in 1968 as "short" and "portly." By that time he had a bald spot on the top of his head. No one at any time has ever described him as Cary Grant handsome.[19]

At Weatherford, Little Joe also acquired his love of music. His sisters played the piano, and the family sang around the piano on holidays. The family's black maid, Lacy, during her baby-sitting chores took him to black places that played the recordings of Jelly Roll Morton, King Oliver, and Louis Armstrong. He went on to love all sorts of music except acid rock, and, in his travels, he developed a habit of reading the local newspapers to see who was playing. He heard the young Roberta Flack, tracked Teddy Wilson, the jazz pianist, around the country, and took his oral history team to hear Charlie Byrd play jazz guitar in Washington, D.C. He played the records of Ella Fitzgerald and Frank Sinatra while he shaved in the morning; he hummed at work; and his daughters thought his lines, "I've got a horse right here, his name is Paul Revere," had been stolen by the composers of *Guys and Dolls*.[20]

Although he had spent some growing-up time elsewhere, it was the small-town culture of Weatherford that most influenced him, for the rest of his life. References continually appeared in his speeches, writings, and correspondence. The comments were not always affectionate. He chafed at the racism and the fact that everyone knew everything that happened. People gossiped, he thought, not for entertainment, but for social censure. When Little Joe was nineteen years old he spotted a black childhood chum, Charles Fred whom he had not seen for about fourteen years, walking on a downtown street. Joe called out tentatively to him. Fred turned, they recognized one another and hugged. They had a wonderful visit, but when Joe got home his mother said that someone had called because they saw Joe hugging a "nigger" downtown. Joe explained that it was Charles Fred, and that he was glad to see him. His mother replied, "Some people in town don't take kindly to your hugging a Negro boy in public." Joe argued, "But, I told you I was glad to see him." Mary Frantz said, "Don't do it anymore. It's just not done."[21]

Joe reflected in 1980, "To my mind, small-town life is overrated unless you are willing to let others make your life for you. . . . Most of the things I have enjoyed for the past forty years, I never heard of until I left Weatherford. My body and my emotions loved the town; my mind and my soul starved for things unknown and unheard of."[22]

Education and raw intelligence gave Little Joe the opportunity to emerge and escape. He went through his sophomore year in high school in Fort Worth and then returned to Weatherford. Geography interested him, and he later told a reporter, "I'm just coasting on what I learned as a seven-year-old."[23] The interest was more than that, however. Frantz always wanted to know where his friends and acquaintances grew up. This was a Southern trait, a matter of identification, of course, but for him it was a part of his interest in people, a way to understand them. It also fed his lust for travel. He read the historical markers on roadways, and played a car game with his children to see who could guess what an upcoming marker would say.[24] On a trip to the eastern shore of Maryland he required me to stop at every Revolutionary War sign, even at night, while he commented on the information illuminated in the circular beam of the headlights.

He had the obsessive impulse of a good travel agent who wants people to get to their destination, not necessarily directly, but by the most interesting route. Even at the end of his rocky third marriage, with his angry wife stomping off to Pennsylvania, he typed out a full-page, single-spaced commentary about various road routes for her to take to Shippensburg.[25] He gave the same sort of unsolicited advice to his daughter Jolie and her new husband, Scott Fleming, about where to go on their honeymoon in Europe. He ended by saying, "I'd better quit, as I am getting all revved up for another trip, and nowhere to go."[26] He wrote to me in 1970, "I presume that you are about to take off for a long safari to Texas [from Colorado] by way of practically everywhere else. Since I do not know your route, I find it slightly difficult to suggest how you should go, but I will make a few sashays at it." He then routed me through the Black Hills, Yellowstone, Salt Lake City, the Grand Canyon, and Albuquerque in order to cover the thousand miles from Fort Collins to Austin—with a wife, three children, and a Siamese cat.[27]

He graduated as valedictorian from Weatherford High School in

1934, and continued at the two-year Weatherford College from 1934 to 1936. He transferred to the University of Texas at Austin and arrived in time to witness a dam break on the Colorado River. He worked as a copy editor and sports reporter for the *Daily Texan*, the campus newspaper, made "A" and "B" grades, and completed a bachelor's degree in journalism, with honors, in 1938. There were few jobs in those late-depression years, but the chair of the journalism department offered a teaching assistantship and commented, "Your fine work as a student last year will be a bright spot in our memory for a long time."[28]

Frantz rejected the offer, and after working briefly for his father in Weatherford he again left home, where there was not enough to do, and became a reporter for the *Temple Daily Telegram*. The reporting job did not last long, and restless, Frantz returned to study history at the University of Texas. "I never made up my mind what profession I wanted to pursue, once I made up my mind that I lacked the arm to play centerfield for the St. Louis Cardinals," he commented.[29] His life was turning toward academics, however, and he wrote a master's thesis, "The Newspapers of the Republic of Texas," under the direction of Eugene C. Barker. At the time, Barker was in his mid-sixties, wore a green eyeshade while he worked, lectured—mainly a recitation of facts—while perched on a high stool, gave high grades, and hated the New Deal.[30]

William C. Binkley, who would later become the editor of the *Journal of Southern History* and the *Mississippi Valley Historical Review*, was teaching summer school at the University of Texas in 1940 and "inherited" the young student for the finish of the thesis. "He educated me in style, depth, and integrity, and I have never written anything since without wondering whether he would find it acceptable. . . . I do believe that I write better because he is continuously looking over my shoulder, at least in a spiritual sense," Frantz later commented.[31]

Phi Theta Kappa Honor Society, Weatherford College. Joe Frantz graduated from Weatherford College in 1936 and married the daughter of the president in 1939. Frantz is second from left in second row. *Photograph from* Weatherford College Yearbook, 1936, *Joe B. Frantz Papers, Center for American History, University of Texas at Austin. CN 10791.*

In 1939, before returning for master's work, Joe married Helen Andrews Boswell, the daughter of the president of Weatherford College. It was a marriage of forty years with two beloved daughters, Jolie and Lisa, that carried him to the pinnacle of his academic career. For most of this time Helen worked as a housewife, keeping Joe on track and, after World War II, helping him with the research for his dissertation.[32] The war, however, interrupted their life as it did for most Americans. He marked time for a year and a half, as the archivist and acting director of the San Jacinto Museum of History in Houston, then, on July 1, 1943, he joined the United States Navy.

His father, a pacifist, wanted him to declare himself a conscientious objector, but Joe decided against this and entered the Navy as an ensign.[33] This was a major break with his father, and a symbolic casting off of the mooring ropes to Weatherford. No longer was he "Little Joe." He went through the Naval Training School at Harvard and completed instruction in communications. He served on three destroyers in the Pacific campaign—*USS Wilkes, HMS Terpsichore,* and *HMS Wager.* He survived seven battle zones including those for the invasion of New Guinea, the second battle of the Philippines, and the occupation of Okinawa. Working often with only three hours sleep he decoded American messages for the British officers to be certain there were no language misunderstandings, and he saw enough combat to quit fearing for his own life.[34] After coming close to death by Japanese bullets, he later claimed, he had no fear of his own death, or for that matter of academic administrators.[35]

After experiencing steaming, raunchy ports, air attacks, long times at sea, and the ocean burial of shipmates, Joe returned to the United States aboard the *USS Wilkes* through the dense fog of Seattle. The sailors eased the blind ship through Puget Sound, and heard Christmas songs drifting through the vapor. "It's heavenly music," said a signalman who knew only curse words. "Listen, it's angels," exclaimed another sailor. All of them cried. Shortly, however, the voice of their own captain bit through the wet, gray embrace, "All right, you bastards, let's get this son-of-a-bitchin' tub tied up and cut out the damned screwing off!"[36] With that jolt of reality, Joe Frantz's war ended.

While at sea, which Frantz described to another seaman as "just miles and miles of miles and miles,"[37] he had been thinking about his future. A letter from Walter Prescott Webb, a professor of history at the University of Texas from whom he had taken a course on the American frontier, advised him:

I think no one but yourself can decide whether you become a museum piece or a historian. It would not, of course, be hard for me to decide, but it is not my life. If you do go into history, then take your degree and do it as soon after the war as possible, because there will then be great demand, one you will not see probably for a long time.[38]

The Navy discharged Lt. (jg) Frantz from Camp Wallace, Texas, on November 23, 1945.[39] Reunited with Helen he returned to the University of Texas and Walter Prescott Webb to complete the graduate work necessary for an academic career. His direction was set.

THE JOURNEY

Walter Prescott Webb was not quite a legend in the late 1940s, but he would become one of the lords of Clio, in part due to the efforts of his most brilliant student, Joe B. Frantz. Webb was a balding, acerbic, cigarette-smoking scholar who had dug his way out of rural Texas ignorance through hard work, education, and the generous financing of a benefactor he never met. He had failed a Ph.D. attempt at the University of Chicago because he did not know enough about Medieval Europe, and because his mind was elsewhere—contemplating the circumstances of migration into the western United States, a trek his family had experienced. Webb returned to Texas from Chicago, gathered his thoughts, and in 1931 published *The Great Plains*, a revolutionary thesis about western settlement.

Webb already had a teaching job at the University of Texas at Austin on the strength of a master's degree and the department's need for a liaison with high school teachers. Webb's mentor, Eugene C. Barker, persuaded him to designate *The Great Plains*, which had won a major prize from Columbia University, as his dissertation for a doctorate at Texas. The history department and the university had the good sense to recognize genius and in 1932 "Dr. Webb," as he became universally known, was promoted to full professor.[1] This man became Joe B. Frantz's mentor, colleague, and friend.

Webb treated his student much as Barker had treated him—he let Frantz follow his own instincts with minimal interference and occasional advice. Frantz chose to write for his dissertation a combination biography and business history of Gail Borden, who invented a method of condensing milk and established an enduring dairy company. Frantz had noted Borden when putting together his master's thesis on Texas newspapers. In his early life Borden had helped start an important Texas newspaper, the *Telegraph and Texas Register* (1835–1877). He was also involved in real estate sales in Galveston and the survey of the City of Houston before making his great success with condensed milk during the time of the Civil War. Frantz completed the dissertation, "Infinite Pursuit: The Story of Gail Borden," in 1948.

Webb gave this advice:

The last part of this Chapter (IX) drags. You have the facts, but you write as if you were tired of G.B. Don't! When tired do something else. . . . Keep in mind that you are portraying a character, painting a picture. . . . Go on now with your story—get all the facts you need—then go off 50 mi. from your notes and revise. Watch those big words—try the simplest ones as Lincoln and the Bible.[2]

Frantz, with support from the Borden Company, pursued an ambition to expand the dissertation into a larger business history of the company. At this point Hines Baker, president of Humble Oil Company, asked both Webb and Professor N. S. B. Gras of Harvard about writing a history of Humble Oil. Gras won the project because Harvard had a business history program. In the conversation, however, Gras mentioned a new Harvard fellowship in business history. Webb, then, asked Frantz if he would be interested in applying, and Joe said, "Sure," without hesitation.

Webb later told Frantz, "I decided right there and then I wanted you on the faculty [at Texas] because you didn't say, 'I'll have to call my wife.'"[3] Such a preemptive attitude would do little to preserve domestic tranquillity today, but the late 1940s was a time when the husband pursued the living, and the wife followed the husband. The post-doctoral fellowship, moreover, would place Frantz nearer the Borden materials and help offset any criticism that all his education came from one institution.

At Harvard, Joe became close friends with the other fellow in the program, Vince Carosso. Together they dreamed about producing a history of American business—even to the point of contacting publishers—but the project became snarled in a proposed rewriting of a skeletal manuscript on business history by Gras, who died in 1956. There were problems with the widow, with credits for authorship, and with freedom to alter the manuscript. The project lingered until 1958, but neither Frantz nor Carosso took it to completion.[4] All writers, of course, have ambitions and books or projects that do not work out. This was the first major one for Frantz, and there would be many others.[5]

Following his year at Harvard, 1948–1949, Joe was able to return to the University of Texas at Austin as a temporary instructor. He had been looking for a teaching position and Webb broached the possibility of a job at Texas. "In your negotiations [with others]," Webb wrote, "it will not hurt to let them know that you have an anchor. Never give a yankee a break, I say."[6] In July, with time running short, Frantz wrote asking about the possibilities in Texas and Webb told him to "sit tight," and write a formal letter about the job. Then on July 23, 1949, Webb, acting as summer chairman, sent Joe an official letter offering a nine-month temporary assistant professorship teaching four courses per semester for $3,500.[7] Webb had convinced the department to give Joe a chance. Frantz thus started teaching at Texas in the fall of 1949.

In 1951 the University of Oklahoma Press brought out Frantz's revised dissertation as *Gail Borden, Dairyman to a Nation*, which received good reviews and a Texas Institute of Letters best book

award. In addition, Frantz began to spin off a series of academic articles and speeches, and learned quickly to increase his academic prestige by first giving a speech or reading a paper, and then seeking its
publication. "The Mercantile House of McKinney & Williams, Underwriters of the Texas Revolution," for example, was first read as a
paper to the Business Historical Society at the American Historical
Association conference in December 1951. It was then published by
the *Bulletin of the Business Historical Society* in March 1952, with off-
prints sent to libraries.[8]

By first reading a paper to an academic audience, scholars can
gain valuable criticism to improve a manuscript before sending it to a
potential publisher. Such action tests the information, brings attention to the scholars and their schools, and informs a home department about the intellectual progress of its members. Moreover, in
the annual audits of faculty both the speech and the publication are
counted—one research effort thus receives double credit. In 1951
the budget council of the Texas history department, the senior voting
body, praised his work and removed the "temporary" from Frantz's
appointment.[9] This meant that he was a fully accepted, tenure-track
member. He was on his way.

Frantz, probably, was the last full-time person in the department
who had earned all of his degrees from the University of Texas at
Austin, which in the 1950s adopted a policy that people should be
hired from the outside, particularly from Ivy League universities.
This would prevent inbreeding, would bring in new ideas, and would
strengthen the department, so it was thought. Webb's degrees had
also all come from Texas, and in his 1958 presidential address to the
American Historical Association he wryly commented: "I am an example of institutional inbreeding which frightens all universities save
the two that practice it most, Harvard and Oxford."[10]

The shift in attitude came with a generational turnover in the
Texas department. When Frantz arrived, there were twenty faculty

members teaching almost four thousand students, with about three-quarters of them in the state-required American history surveys. The focus of the "Old Department" had been on training teachers and master's degree work. Milton R. Gutsch, chairman from 1928 to 1951, was the advisor for all of the graduate students. He retired in 1951, however, as did Eugene C. Barker, who had been on reduced service since 1945. Webb reached mandatory retirement age in 1958, but continued to teach on a part-time basis. A new generation—including Oliver H. Radkey, Barnes F. Lathrop, William R. Braisted, Robert C. Cotner, H. Bailey Carroll, T. Harry Bennett, Archibald R. Lewis, Thomas F. McGann, John Sunder, and Joe B. Frantz—took over the department in the 1950s.[11]

An emphasis on training Ph.D. research scholars took hold, and as more outside faculty members with outside interests arrived, faculty interest in Texas history waned to the point that, in the 1960s, Texas history was dropped as a Ph.D. field. Frantz, who readily progressed through the academic ranks (assistant professor, 1949–1953; associate professor, 1953–1959; full professor, 1959–1986), was a witness to these changes and chairman of the department from 1959 to 1965. He pointed out to a colleague at Stephen F. Austin State College that students demanded greater rigor, and that the university had raised its GRE scores from 800 to 1100. He observed that there were lots of "A's" and "F's" as good students were rewarded and poor students were eliminated, that growth was exponential, and that classes were being scheduled at night and on Saturdays. "The result is we look like one big factory teeming with activity," he said, "for the past four or five years this place has lost all appearance of leisureliness."[12]

In addition, the old custom of exchanging faculty in the summertime came to an end. Frantz had benefited as a master's student when William C. Binkley came to Austin for the summer. As a Texas faculty member Frantz, somewhat anachronistically, taught during

Room 104, Garrison Hall. Frantz's office at the University of Texas was next door to his mentor Walter Prescott Webb. They drank coffee, joked, and traveled together. Following Webb's death Frantz inherited the mantle of Texas history that had passed from Eugenc C. Barker to Webb. *Photograph from UT Student Publications, Center for American History, University of Texas at Austin. CN 09046.*

various summers as a visiting professor at Utah State University, Northwestern University, Southern Methodist University Research Center in Taos, the University of Maine, the University of Colorado, and Corpus Christi State University. Historian Thomas Brewer, who wrote about the "Old Department," reasoned that the faculty was not particularly interested in graduate education and, wishing to escape the students in the summer, they imported distinguished professors.[13] For Joe B., who sought summer teaching throughout his career, it seems more a means to gather some income and scratch his chronic itch of wanderlust. It appears, moreover, that this summertime game of academic musical chairs was widespread in the nation—after all, the distinguished professors came from the history departments of other universities. The custom disappeared as younger faculty members demanded the summer teaching income, and older professors who had enough money chose to do something besides teach.

Of the older members, Walter Prescott Webb alone remained active in the department after official retirement. Webb continued his university work into the early 1960s. His office, Room 102, on the first floor of Garrison Hall in the center of the campus was in a choice position, across the tile foyer from the departmental administrative offices. Frantz was housed next door to Webb in Room 104. They drank "a world of coffee" together, Joe said, and developed a father-son relationship without the "tender overtones." They embarked on various adventures during which the student absorbed wisdom and attitude from his famous mentor. A two-day trip to Kingsville for a commencement address, for example, turned into a five-day excursion—to Corpus Christi to visit a former Austin newspaperman, to Victoria to see the antiques in the Denver Hotel, to Galveston because Webb wanted to experience the nightclub entertainment of the Balinese Room, and finally back to Austin.[14] "He [Webb] enjoyed the fact that I didn't need to make any plans,"

Frantz recalled. It was a time when Webb talked a lot and the young colleague listened and absorbed.[15]

The master listed three necessities for writers: a belief that they had something to say, a conviction that what they had to say was worth saying, and a certainty that they could say it better than anyone else. If a person came to doubt these, Webb claimed, the writer "immediately loses that confidence and self deception . . . so essential to authorship."[16] Webb wrote little for the professional journals, and more for newspapers and popular magazines, *Harper's* to *True West*. He advised Joe:

> The public is not interested in highly technical recitals and there is a place for someone to put this technical information into the language of the people. Moreover, I hope that you will set up your own objectives and follow through without much regard to the opinion of experts, even myself. I think we work best when we work in harmony with what is inside us rather than outside us.[17]

The venerated old man also gave an antidote for pomposity, the occupational disease of academics:

> Whenever I get to feeling like I'm somebody—and I recommend this for any University man who gets to feeling like a big-shot bastard—I go to San Antonio and stand on that busy corner outside the Gunter Hotel for an hour and just watch the people go by and ask myself how many of all those persons ever heard of Walter Webb or ever gave one thought to the University of Texas in a day's time, or even cared whether the University exists or goes to hell. That puts things back in perspective.[18]

And he practiced intergenerational generosity—helping younger people along, with the confidence that they in turn would help the next generation. Webb himself had been aided by a stranger, William E. Hinds of Brooklyn, who answered the plea of an unknown boy in faraway Texas for books, magazines, and the chance for an education. Frantz heard, in addition, the story of John Haller, a poor English student during World War II who desperately needed a place to live.

Webb took the student to an empty, small frame house he owned on the outskirts of Austin and told Haller he could live there. When asked about the rent, Webb replied, "Nothing. How do you think I can charge you? You are just beginning, I've already lived my life."[19] As Webb's friend, the southwestern folklorist, J. Frank Dobie, observed, "Men who keep gratitude in their hearts for a lifetime and want to pay inner debts that nobody else knows about do not run in herds."[20]

The friendship deepened between Webb and Frantz in the fourteen years their offices were side by side in Garrison Hall. Webb bought a ranch, Friday Mountain, near Austin and moved old cabins to it in a spirit of historic preservation, or "fool stunts" as he expressed it. "Since you left," he wrote to Joe in a summer letter, "I have bought a new car, Plymoth [sic], and another log cabin. I can't spell Plymouth, but I can spell cabbin [sic]. The car was reasonable, but the cabin was outrageous."[21]

Webb, a shy, blunt man, did not brag, or extol his own brilliance, or seek honors, or try to move from the University of Texas. He was content in Austin. Although Webb did not participate in the administration of national historical groups, Frantz enjoyed that sort of work, and began in 1951 to trumpet his mentor for high office.[22] No matter how brilliant, nonparticipants will not gain much recognition without someone on the inside promoting them. Webb thus became head of the Mississippi Valley Historical Association (now the Organization of American Historians) in 1954 and the American Historical Association in 1958.

Webb was president of the MVHA when the program chairman, Lewis E. Atherton of the University of Missouri, became ill. Webb appointed Joe to take over as acting chair for the St. Louis convention. There were thirty sessions with two dinner speakers—Webb and Harry S Truman. Twenty-four hours before he was scheduled to talk, Truman casually cancelled because of other obligations. "The execu-

tive council of the association panicked, the Hotel Jefferson panicked, the food suppliers and waiters' union panicked, I panicked,"
Joe stated.

He worked without success to find a substitute—who could re-
place Truman? There was fear that the cancellation would bankrupt
the association. Someone shouted, "That little son-of-a-bitch has just
wrecked his place in history!" But, Anheuser-Busch came to the rescue by inviting the convention to the brewery for free beer and Gay
90's entertainment. By ten o'clock that night people had forgiven
the association and forgotten Truman. History survived, and Joe
Frantz was a hero.[23]

When Webb reached retirement age in 1958, Frantz put together a series of his shorter essays with a long introductory biographical
sketch of Webb for Houghton-Mifflin. Joe based his sketch on personal knowledge and the reponse of various friends to a letter of in-
quiry. "I do not intend to gild the lily, because I think he is so much
more attractive in his unvarnished, grumpy state," Frantz wrote.
Frantz offered no footnotes in this introduction. Yet, there is a rough
consensus that "An Appreciative Introduction" at the beginning of
An Honest Preface is the best writing Joe Frantz ever produced. Rodman Paul, a highly respected mining historian from the California Institute of Technology, wrote Joe, "With [your] Dobie [obituary in
American West], as with your ever more memorable article on Webb
in *An Honest Preface*, you've given us a speaking picture, not just a
commemoration ode. It makes it easier for us who are not Texans to
know these men in a meaningful way. Many thanks."[24] Frantz also
liked his characterization of Webb, and wrote an inscription to an
undesignated person on the overleaf of a copy, "A labor of love that
surprisingly got used in many graduate seminars in historiography . . .
I have been rather pleased with this."[25]

Everyone in the department, including Joe B., watched with
warm interest, titillation, and gossip as the seventy-three-year-old,

shy, crusty widower, Walter Webb, began to court the irrepressible, sixty-year-old widow, Terrell Maverick of San Antonio. Webb blossomed like a cactus flower, wrote love letters, and roamed the hallways like a "star-struck sophomore."[26] He attended an opera in San Antonio with her and commented in awe, "I never saw anything like it—she kissed her way all across that auditorium lobby!"[27] Frantz teased his mentor, "Dr. Webb, there's a rumor going around that you and Mrs. Maverick are going to *have* to get married," to which Webb replied with good humor, "You son-of-a-bitch."[28] They married late in 1961, and Webb told his friend Dobie, "This was an unexpected dividend from life."[29]

The happiness ended abruptly and tragically, however, in 1963. In a one-car accident on Interstate 35 near Buda, Webb rolled his Plymouth three times and died instantly. Terrell, asleep at the time with her head on her husband's lap, woke in the glare of emergency-room lights and heard someone mention "D.O.A." Joe went to Austin's Brackenridge Hospital to comfort Terrell, who was badly injured. "He's dead, isn't he?" she asked when he entered the room. "Yes," Joe replied. She said reflectively, "But God, didn't I give him fourteen months on the mountain top!"[30]

Frantz had lost his most important mentor and friend. He shared Webb's intellectual zest for the interplay of geography, people, and history. Webb had seen in this talented younger colleague the person to inherit the mantle of Texas history that had passed from Eugene C. Barker, biographer of Stephen F. Austin, to himself. "Naturally, I would like for you to remain at Texas," the older man wrote in 1956 when Frantz was contemplating an outside job offer, "because I think you represent Texas in the University better than anyone else in the department. I happen to think Texas is of some importance, even in a university."[31] With Webb's death the cloak of Texas history passed on to embrace the shoulders of the younger man—from Barker to Webb to Frantz.

At this point Frantz was chairman of a department that was in the process of becoming a powerful doctoral unit. He was not so much an instigator of change—there is little evidence of curriculum reform, for example, during his reign—as he was a colleague taking a turn as helmsman of an academic boat rushing along in a torrent of university evolution and expansion. The position of chair gave him, however, a secretarial staff and access to the higher reaches of the administration. In addition, he inherited from Webb an ongoing program to film the great historians of the period talking about their ideas.

"American Civilization by Its Interpreters" was a project funded by the Ford Foundation to videotape twenty masters of the profession in thirty-minute lectures on American history from 1492 to the present. It was an early experiment in teaching by television, and Webb had completed about one-fourth of the venture when he died. Unfortunately, Webb himself had not been recorded. The department granted Frantz released time to complete the enterprise, and in the mid-1960s the university broadcasted the course to seven universities around Texas.[32] Historiography is rarely of much interest to undergraduates, but the chance to see current great historians talking about their ideas was a blessing for graduate students. For Joe it was an early lesson in oral history and an opportunity to meet the leaders of the profession. He maintained these important contacts with letters and greetings at conventions. This all enhanced his own reputation and provided a network of powerful professional friends beyond Texas.

Webb and Frantz, in addition, had planned a picture book about the American West. They had signed a contract with the Macmillan Company, and had begun to gather photographs. Frantz had even written Walt Disney Productions in the search for pictures, and said: "Walter P. Webb is generally conceded to be the most significant writer in the field of Western America. His reputation is international. I am just a tail to his kite and only reasonably insignificant, or significant, as you choose."[33] The picture book failed; it was never completed.

The shadow of Webb, however, did not quickly fade away. Frantz gave speeches and wrote articles about his famous mentor, and planned a biography. When historian Walter Rundell Jr. wanted to write a book about Webb, he was blocked by Frantz's exclusive rights to the Webb papers housed at the Barker Texas History Center. Neither scholar completed the work—Frantz did not even begin to write it, and Rundell died suddenly at age fifty-three in 1982.[34]

Necah Stewart Furman, however, a graduate student at the University of New Mexico, wrote a dissertation on Webb, which was published by the University of New Mexico Press in 1976 as *Walter Prescott Webb: His Life and Impact*. She utilized the papers at the Barker Texas History Center, and Frantz wrote an introduction to the book. Joe B. does not "star" in the text, and although he was quoted at times, his long, intimate friendship with Webb was not mined. This raises questions without answers—did Frantz withhold information or not take the book seriously; did he harbor ambitions to write the story himself; did the author and her mentors suppress Frantz's role?[35] Nonetheless, the Furman book is a sound piece of scholarship and the only Webb biography that exists.

Webb's influence in Austin and at the University of Texas was also commemorated with the "Webb Symposium" of 1972. Cecil Bernard ("C.B.") Smith Sr., a former Webb student and successful Ford automobile dealer in Austin, and Maj. Jubal Richard ("J.R.") Parten, Houston oilman and University of Texas regent, along with the university financed an "International Symposium in Honor of Walter Prescott Webb." Frantz was appointed chair of the organizing committee and sent out invitations presenting the purpose of the conference: "It is our thought to bring together some of the most talented and thoughtful people in the world under circumstances

Frantz organized the Webb Symposium with the idea that if you brought great minds together, then great ideas would emerge. As it worked out the great intellects had a hard time communicating with anyone outside their field of expertise and only chaos emerged. From left to right: JBF, Rodney Kidd, C. B. Smith Sr., Stephen Spurr. *Photograph from Joe B. Frantz Papers, Center for American History, University of Texas at Austin. CN 10787.*

that would encourage each to address himself to those matters that most deeply concern him about life on this planet."[36]

The meeting featured a group of recognized intellects such as Daniel Bell, sociologist; Raymond Aron, philosopher; Aaron Copland, composer; Loren Eiseley, anthropologist; Alfred Kazin, literary critic; Sol Linowitz, diplomat; Nathaniel Owings, architect; and Herman Kahn, physicist. The core group of thirty-three also included a group of bright young people from a variety of disciplines, to challenge the statements of the giants. In addition, there were over a hundred observers, all meeting on the top floor of the LBJ Library.

Frantz told me at the time that the main thought was to throw a

The Webb Symposium. From left to right: JBF, Harry Ransom, Bentley Glass, Herman Kahn. *Photograph from Joe B. Frantz Papers, Center for American History, University of Texas at Austin. CN 10786.*

lot of smart people together and see what would happen. It was an interesting idea, but essentially nothing happened because the participants were all divergent specialists talking their own language. They spoke in lofty skewed lines that neither collided nor triggered much reaction in anybody else. Copland, for example, had to ask the meaning of "GNP," and Kazin needed an explanation of "factor of two." Robert Reinhold of the *New York Times* commented that the conference was a "Texas grandiosity," much too broad and lacking direction of thought. Nobody listened.[37] At the concluding dinner H. Max Gluckman, the British anthropologist, was supposed to sum up the meaning of the conference. He stood up, announced it was impossible, and instead offered a toast to the Queen.[38]

The Webb Symposium, though it failed to accomplish much, did no harm to Frantz's career. He was a genial host, and his position as Webb's successor was confirmed.[39] Frantz, moreover, had already followed his mentor into the position of director of the Texas State Historical Association. The TSHA, which claimed to be the oldest learned society in Texas, began in 1897 and published the academic journal, *Southwestern Historical Quarterly*. It was a nonprofit organization sheltered by the University of Texas at Austin; the director had to be a member of the university faculty. The director was also in charge of the Center for Studies in Texas History, funded by the university for the encouragement of research. Barker was the director from 1911 to 1937, and Webb from 1937 to 1946. H. Bailey Carroll succeeded Webb, and when he died in 1966, Joe B. Frantz became director upon the insistence of Harry Ransom, a legendary chancellor of the University of Texas System. Frantz bargained for an assistant director and remained as director until 1977.

In this position he pushed to completion volume three of the *Handbook of Texas*, a supplement of new material and corrections to the original encyclopedic *Handbook*; began *Riding Line*, the membership newsletter; started a summer institute in Texas studies for teachers; added book exhibits to the annual meeting of the association; and founded the Webb Historical Society, an historical club for university and college students. Frantz brought enthusiasm and vigor to the rather stagnant association, and with the aid of TSHA president Fred Cotten of Weatherford opened the door to young scholars with added sessions at the annual convention.[40]

His most dramatic alteration, with ensuing altercations, came to the *Southwestern Historical Quarterly*. The earlier journal presented its table of contents on a staid, green front cover. It was also known for sloppy documentation with a touch of cronyism in its publication. Joe changed this by hiring Carl Hertzog, a printer from El Paso, along with José Cisneros, an artist from El Paso, to redesign the cover and lettering. With the help of L. Tuffly Ellis, his tough, new

As director of the Texas State Historical Association from 1966 to 1977 Frantz published the third volume of the *Handbook of Texas* (first edition), revised the *Southwestern Historical Quarterly*, and expanded the annual meeting of the association. *Photograph from Joe B. Frantz Papers, Center for American History, University of Texas at Austin. CN 10788.*

assistant director, a modern *Quarterly* emerged in July 1967 with a full-color painting on its cover. The cover changed with each issue, the table of contents was placed inside, and the book reviews were listed in rough chronological order, rather than in the more idiosyncratic order of the editor's favored authors or reviewers. Ellis insisted upon originality and the proper documentation of articles, and sent them out to readers in the field for evaluation before publication.

The flash of color on the cover and the higher standards of scholarship ruffled the feathers of the conservative, older birds of the profession in Texas, but the changes remained.[41] The younger birds liked it. Marilyn McAdams Sibley, a future president of the TSHA, wrote, "The July issue of the *Quarterly* is so excellent in every respect

—concept, design, illustration, and prose—that it brought a lump to my throat."[42] The *Southwestern Historical Quarterly* and the Texas State Historical Association had thus been nudged by Frantz and his staff to a higher professional level.

Frantz, meanwhile, also succeeded in two other major areas of a professor's life—teaching and publication. Lecturing in business history and American history, Joe became a popular instructor, even for eight o'clock Saturday morning classes. His office door was usually wide open, and he did not mind interruptions. His style was anecdotal, and he frequently used stories to make a point. As time went by his storehouse of historical vignettes became endless, and he used these in and out of class, in speeches, and in conversation.

Joe was a superb storyteller. He depended upon his memory and needed few classroom notes. He would sit at times like a Buddha, on a table with eyes half-closed, and lecture.[43] During his later years, at Corpus Christi State University, a student wrote on a class evaluation about what she liked: "The way Dr. Frantz teaches. He just sits [crosslegged] on top of the desk, and the information just flows out of his mouth. He makes everything very interesting."[44] A final-exam question in his modern American history course asked students to "Analyze whether in the years after the Great Society the United States has advanced or retreated in the quality of living as a result of the Reagan Revolution. Use examples. Show some passion! Be vindictive! Rave on! Get it off your chest!"[45] Who could not like such a teacher?

At the University of Texas, in 1955 Frantz received a grant to attend a Ford Foundation Educational Forum, in 1957 he won the Lemuel Scarbrough Faculty Award for excellence in teaching, and in 1959 he arranged for a student exhange with Chile. Frantz was elected to a seat on the national board of Phi Alpha Theta, the history honorary society, in 1955. This led to a vice presidency in 1961, and the presidency for two years, 1963–1964. In 1964 a student pep

As a young faculty member Frantz expended an unusual amount of energy in teaching. His lectures were filled with anecdotes, his office door was open to students, and he welcomed interruptions. At the Honor's Day reception in 1957, he received a major teaching award, the Lemuel Scarbrough Faculty Award, from the University of Texas. Helen Frantz, his wife, is shown on the left; Paul Thompson is on the right. *Photograph from Joe B. Frantz Papers, Center for American History, University of Texas at Austin. CN 10785.*

group, the Cowboys, made him an honorary member and gave him a certificate and a neckerchief. These achievements indicate his success on the undergraduate level of teaching. "As a history teacher," he said, "I want to make students aware of the various aspects of the past which have conditioned them—which have brought them to where they are and which have made them what they are, and which point the way they may be going."[46]

There was a different sort of response, less enthusiastic, from his graduate students. When I arrived in Austin for registration in fall 1962, for example, I met Dr. Frantz for the first time as he was sorting books in his Garrison office. He was preoccupied, but the door was open so I introduced myself. I was coming for Ph.D. work in business history with him and had been recommended by Professor Louis Galambos of Rice. I expected some recognition, but all I got was a rather disinterested "Hummmf." I told my friend Tom Charlton, now the vice provost for research at Baylor University, about this and Tom, who had worked with Webb and knew Frantz, said, "Aw, he acts that way every now and then. Don't worry about it."

Having already studied business history with Galambos and already with an M.B.A., I didn't get much of anything new from Frantz's business history seminar. And then it came to the dissertation. I had planned to do something about the extraction of mineral resources from the sea and had published an article about desalinization. At that point I found a new book on my proposed topic. Frantz's retort about this situation was, "Can you do it better?" This is something Webb would have said. I doubted that I could, and suggested instead that I write a history of Houston, my hometown. Frantz said, "Well, I was thinking of that myself, but you go ahead." He knew Dr. Allen Going, the chairman of history at the University of Houston, and arranged a job for me as an instructor at Houston, where I would be near my source materials. He told me to go to work and follow my own instincts. Two years later I presented him with a finished manuscript, none of which he had seen. His mouth dropped a bit when I plopped down the five hundred pages of typescript, and he growled, "If any graduate student ever presents a whole dissertation to me again like this, I'm going to burn it in front of him!" I took that as a joke and an accolade.

He read the material, made very few comments, and told me to take it to Frank Wardlaw at the University of Texas Press for consideration of publication. The press published the book in short order, and Frantz, I thought, had had little to do with it, other than giving me license to work, leaving me alone, and opening a few doors. At that point I had not learned much from him in an academic sense, and did not have enough sense to realize what had been done. Barker had left Webb alone to develop and find his way; Webb had let Frantz seek his own path; Frantz treated me, and others, with the same think-and-swim independence. It was an unappreciated gift. Ronald L. Davis, one of his earlier graduate students, actually sought out Frantz as a director because of his openness to student interests, and experienced much the same sort of treatment.[47] As Davis and I, and others, would find out later, the real teaching from Joe B. Frantz came afterwards with his continued friendship and association.

At this time—the fifties, sixties, and early seventies—before the market for historians closed down, the "old boy" network was operating. If a department chairman needed an instructor, he would call a colleague elsewhere to see if someone was available. In like manner, a major professor might call a friend to see if there was a job opening. There were no Office of Economic Opportunity restrictions, and I had benefited by obtaining a job at the University of Houston where I could both support my family and work on my dissertation. For better or worse, it was the way the profession worked at the time.

Frantz, with a large network of friends and contacts, was an ideal job source for a young graduate, and he remembered his students as opportunities arose. "Would you be interested in moving to OU at the associate professor level? You would undoubtedly be expected to teach and direct considerable Western history, but if your studies of Texas cities doesn't acquaint you with the West, what will?" he wrote to me in 1973.[48] He wrote Ronnie Davis in 1964, "Would you be interested in an assistant professorship at UCLA at a maximum of $7,700. You would definitely have to declare on the side of Western history. Let me hear pronto." Davis replied, "Of course, I'd be interested in an assistant professorship at UCLA—at any price."[49] What this sort of interchange meant was that Frantz would put your name

Frantz had an enormous capacity for friendship. Loquacious, humorous, and outgoing he is shown here at the annual meeting of the Texas State Historical Association in 1971 with William C. Pool (center) of Southwest Texas State University, and W. Eugene Hollon of the University of Toledo. Frantz and Hollon delighted in humorously insulting one another during introductions at academic meetings. *Photograph from Texas State Historical Association collection.*

in the job pot with a strong recommendation. Sometimes a job would materialize, and sometimes not, but it was gratifying that your major professor had not forgotten you.

At professional meetings Frantz would often stand in the lobby of the convention hotel and introduce his students to the scholars who came up to greet him. Tuffly Ellis once noticed him in New York with his leg propped up on the wall talking, and, three hours later, found him still there, talking, greeting, introducing.[50] He would often follow your career until you were reasonably well placed and then he would back off to let you flourish or wilt as you would. He nudged Ronnie Davis along the road through Emporia State and

Michigan State, finally introducing him to a scholar at Southern Methodist University where Davis finally stuck. Along the way he commented to Ronnie, one of his favorite students:

> Needless to say, I am proud of you. You are rapidly reaching that stage where you don't require much of me, but as before, if there is any door that you can't pry open and maybe I can help, don't hesitate to fall back. You will never get so old and great and experienced, however, that there won't be someone at least older and with a special *entree* to some situation; so use whoever it is. And at the same time, remember that you are, in the eyes of the people still in graduate school, much more successful than you think you are, and so keep an eye out for something you can do for some of them along the way. It can be a very satisfying profession, because you can develop to a great extent along the lines you would like to, and at the same time, amid all the drudges and lackluster types you will encounter, you will get very close to some wonderful people who will at times be exhilarating if not downright exciting. And that goes for anybody from undergraduates to the elder statesmen. It's also a good profession for dreaming.[51]

Such letters are treasured, and help validate the choice of a career. And it was in such acts of friendship, support, and mentoring that Frantz succeeded best in the realm of teaching, that part of a professor's life that burns up one-third to one-half of his time.

There was another solid reason for Webb's faith in his former student—Frantz's success in publication. In 1954 Savoie Lottinville, editor of the University of Oklahoma Press, which had published *Gail Borden*, wrote to Frantz about a collaboration with Julian E. Choate Jr., who had sent the press a manuscript, "The Myth of the American Cowboy." Choate was an English professor at David Lipscomb College in Nashville, and the manuscript was his dissertation at Vanderbilt. He had grown up as a farm and ranch boy, and knew what he was writing about. Lottinville, however, thought the material was disorganized, humorless, and repetitious. "The man is too grim," said the editor to Frantz. "You can give the manuscript the sparkle it needs." The editor introduced the two scholars by letter, and Frantz reworked the material. The book came out in 1955 as

The American Cowboy: The Myth and the Reality, an analysis of cowboy life in history, fiction, and folklore.[52]

Frantzian sparkles are abundant—"Given a southerner with in-bred equestrianism, a saddle a man could stick to, a lariat, and a double-cinched mustang who knew as much about a longhorn as his rider, and you had the tools for an industry, the tools to work and mold the resource, the Texas longhorn."[53] And, "When the movie fades out on wings of song and the first kiss, its maker shows his sagacity in sparing his audience, for the years ahead of the sweet young calicoed thing are likely to be grim and wearing and unrelieved."[54]

Webb reviewed the book for the *Austin American Statesman* and said, "I couldn't find any place to lay it down. . . ."[55] But *Time* magazine mocked the "vicarious vaqueros" in an unsigned review that ended in a poem:

> Ah'm an ole Phi Bete
> From the Lone Star State
> Ma pard's Ph.D.
> Out o' Tennessee
> We tote no guns and we rob no stages
> We punch no cows and we bank our wages
> But we sure ride herd on them Eng. Lit. majors
> Yippeeyi Oklahoma U.[56]

Frantz admitted later that *Time* had torn "the hide off my back," but wrote soothingly to Choate at the time, "I got a good deal of amusement out of it and feel a little like the actress who didn't care what scandalous things were printed about her so long as they spelled her name right."[57] Savoie Lottinville consoled them with a report of good sales, and advice to ignore that "smart-aleck stuff" in *Time*. He assured them they would be quoted for the next quarter century.[58] At the end of the twentieth century the book is still a standard, listed in the bibliographies for the cowboy era in American history.

A similar book opportunity, one that would bring less acrimony, followed shortly when Frank Wardlaw, director of the University of Texas Press, encouraged a collaboration with Cordia Sloan Duke of Dalhart. As a young school teacher in 1907 Cordia married Robert L. Duke, the last manager of the XIT Ranch, one of the largest in the world. Sensing a passing era she kept a diary in her apron pocket and persuaded various cowboys to sit down and write about their experiences. She collected around eighty memoirs, and in 1957 thought about publishing them. According to Frantz, when they met "it was love at first sight," and it was agreed that the professor would put together the book. Joe arranged the chapters, edited a bit, added some spice, and the result was *6,000 Miles of Fence: Life on the XIT Ranch of Texas,* published by the University of Texas Press in 1961.[59] The book was well received. "A work of rare insight into life at the grass roots," wrote Wayne Gard for the *Dallas News.*[60]

This effort along with *The American Cowboy* established Frantz as a Texas and western historian, a reputation he carried for the rest of his life. It is interesting, however, that in both cases it was someone else—Choate or Duke—who had done the hard basic research, the time-consuming, patient gathering of information. This became Joe's writing pattern—to make interesting what others had done and to rely on secondary sources. Although he was capable of grinding research, as in the case of *Gail Borden,* his talent with words, his genius for turning a phrase, came to dominate his work. It may well be that this gift was too great, and that he relied on it too much in a busy life. More than one interviewee for this book has commented that he could have been a really "great" historian if he had not depended so much upon the clever quip. Perhaps, but what is "great"?

Eugene Hollon, a western historian and close friend, commented:

The man's writing style is as original and free as his spirit. . . . Few individuals are born with a natural talent for writing. For most it remains a painful struggle to avoid over use of passive verbs, trite alliterations, misplaced commas, and overworked cliches. . . . Then along comes a man like Joe Frantz who violates everything I have preached against for decades—not to mention every rule in a publisher's manual of style. Joe's sentences (more often non-sentences) can give a high school teacher apoplexy. Yet, who would be foolish enough to tamper with a unique, pithy style that has become his trademark? Certainly not me![61]

As a brief example of what Frantz could do, consider this commentary on Alonso Álvarez de Pineda for the fledgling *Sand Dollar Watch Magazine* at Port Isabel in 1976. Not much is known about Pineda whose exploration of the Gulf Coast in 1519 is mentioned only in the summary of a royal grant of territory. Here is what Frantz made out of that scrap of information:

No matter. We can reconstruct, and we can argue the reconstruction. After all, this is the stuff of which history is made. The kind of controversy and uncertainty keeps history vital, moving, and occasionally revisionist. This is what keeps history from being what is sometimes charged, a simple movement of a set of bones from one graveyard to another.

What really matters here is the fact that Pineda, his associates, and his successors stimulated people to explore this part of the world, to come back and check on their predecessors, to try to claim a little more, with concomitantly, a little more certainty. Pineda stimulated competitiveness. Whether he sailed up the Rio Grande or the Mississippi, he caused other men to want to sail in this direction.

As generations and centuries went by this part of the world became settled. . . . One day the Spaniards came north overland from Mexico proper, and crossed these shores not too far from where this is being published. At some low tide Spanish cattle crossed, to move up into brush country around the Nueces, giving birth to the range cattle industry which would provide Texas a new chapter and a romantic tradition, and would rescue it from its economic impoverishment following the Civil War.

Here Juan Cortina played both sides of the river, giving later people a folk-hero unmatched by most other recognizable regions of this nation. . . . Here a war with Mexico was launched, and a future President, Zachary Taylor, was uncovered. Here, or across from here, men plotted one of the great continuing movements of the twentieth century, the Mexican Revolution.

Here, Texas versions of Rhett Butler made fortunes, running blockades to deliver cotton and arms in a hopeless cause. Into here came that Scottish cowboy, Ewen Cameron, to march on Mier and to get himself shot on orders from no less than Antonio Lopez de Santa Anna. Here too, when citizens and black troops got at cross purposes, occurred that unbelievable sequence during which local people demanded that the blacks be removed, and President Theodore Roosevelt replied by removing Fort Brown from the War Department to the Department of Interior, where it became an experimental garden for spineless cactus. What a formula—spirited citizens plus spirited soldiers produce spineless cactus.

And from here hot-eyed promoters and speculators traveled northward to sell unseen land to incredibly credulous farmers in Iowa, Minnesota, and other states. They bought land then like they buy religion and insurance from Del Rio today—or goat herd masculinity, a few years ago. They bought, believing that God had intended this country for a garden, not of spineless cacti, but rich with fruits and vegetables. Once here, they learned that cliche about Texas, like Hell, needing only water to make the desert bloom. Faced with ruin, they found water, and the desert did flower, the Valley did become the Winter Garden of the United States, sending its trucks of produce rumbling north with succulence at a time when every place else is stripped bare with cold and the people are shivering from sunless days. From here came that pink grapefruit known and treasured throughout the world.

All these things Pineda did. He brought history to the Rio Grande Valley. Whatever the details, he first gave notice to the outside world that here was a region to explore, to learn about, possibly to live in.[62]

Recognizing that there was little to say about Pineda, and that there was disagreement about the facts, Frantz used sweeping statements about the history after Pineda to indicate his importance as a pathfinder. There was really nothing new in what he wrote. But, Frantz said it dramatically with the use of colorful, descriptive words— "Texas versions of Rhett Butler made fortunes," and "trucks of produce rumbling north with succulence," and "when every place else is stripped bare with cold and the people are shivering from sunless days." A writer of less imagination would have said, "Texas entrepreneurs," and "trucks sent north with fruit," and "when every place else suffers winter."

In 1971, for another example, I wrote the basic manuscript for *Houston: A Students' Guide to Localized History*, a minor publication, and Frantz polished it to send to the Teachers College Press at

Columbia University.[63] At one point I said: "Like many other town promoters the Allens enthusiastically pushed their enterprise, and like others they might have failed, except that Houston occupied an advantageous place at a fortuitous time." Frantz changed the sentence to read: "Like many other town promoters the Allens enthusiastically pushed their enterprise, and they might have failed, *except that Houston became a product of happy timing—it occupied the right place at the right time in history* [italics mine]."[64] My version was technically correct and efficient and dull; his version was also correct, but readable and interesting. It had his magic spark—a tweak of words, the touch of his genius.

Throughout his writings—books, book reviews, chapters of anthologies, book introductions, letters—you can see the spark. It can be seen in his use of words and phrases—anecdotal, pithy, bawdy at times, reminiscent, Texan, unexpected, humorous, provocative. The following examples should be read slowly, even read aloud, and enjoyed like fine eighteen-year-old, single malt Scotch whisky. Pause, the purpose here is not to become drunk on the prose, or dizzy with fast reading, but rather to enjoy the complex flavor and employment of a wide-ranging mind. Savor the words. It is a glimpse beyond mere information into one of insight and feeling.

In the [farm] country a person learns how to wait, learns that some things can't be rushed, and some things have to be endured. . . . The most wonderful morning sound is that of the rooster. But if the rooster is your alarm clock, you hate him.[65]

'Will You Come to the Bower I Have Shaded for You' . . . not exactly a martial air, but a pleasant thought for a Sunday afternoon.[66]

From the 1820s to 1861 Sam Houston was like a larger than life stink bug in America's life. No matter how many times you plugged his hole and pressed him down, he always reappeared somewhere else, as tangible a factor as ever.[67]

To southwesterners the Alamo ranks alongside Lexington and Concord, Saratoga, and Cowpens. The shots there may not have been heard around the world, but they were certainly heard from Mexico City across Texas to

Washington, and that covers enough distance to assure that the men who fell there would be remembered.[68]

For Texas was planted in poverty, nurtured in rock-hard soil, and has endured and matured on alternating diets of plenty and famine, spiced with most of the dirty tricks that a frequently hostile Nature knows how to play.[69]

Here then is the Holy Trinity of Texas. What the cod and fisherman and God meant to New England, the mustang, longhorn, and cowboy meant to Texas. They symbolized a freedom which probably never really existed, but which people like to think existed.[70]

What really hurts about Texas, lies in what it could be, against what it is.[71]

To outsiders Texans aren't people, but bizarre creatures with underdeveloped brains, overdeveloped appetites, and a penchant for violence that never wanes.[72]

Texas is 12 million people who are bright and dumb, conservative and liberal, tall and short and slim and fat, courageous and cowardly—just like the people in Connecticut and Oregon.[73]

In a world that often shows signs of weariness, I personally often wish that Texas would grow up—but only a little bit. It is too much like an enthusiastic Dalmation that smothers you with affection and cannot understand why you don't think it is the greatest dog in the world.[74]

We need one more burial in Dallas. We need to bury the old myth. And we need to nurture a new myth—that while Texans appreciate the good and evil of the past, primarily Texans and Southwesterners are in league with the future, determined to create a world in which fact and purpose and aspiration can live side by side. Some sniper [Lee Harvey Oswald] has handed us an opportunity—clean cut and real. Either we seize it to build on, or we rejoin the world as the overgrown, bullying, cry-babies it thinks we are. I vote for the building program.[75]

Yellowstone [National Park] started something. Ever since, men have tried to safeguard some of the best of what is, and what has been, even though it has meant giving quality priority over profit. Using Yellowstone as a starting block, we have been groping toward cooperating with our environment instead of forever and inflexibly demanding its unconditional surrender to our short-tempered and temporary needs and demands. . . . In 1972 [the centennial of the park] it points the way for crowded mankind to take his elbow from between his neighbor's ribs. Even if only for a moment, man needs to know that somewhere, some time, he can now and then breathe.[76]

The rutted trails [of the West] needed few markers other than the carcasses of oxen, broken wagon wheels, jettisoned furniture, and graves, graves, graves. People had accidents, women died in childbirth for want of sanitation and their babies for lack of mothering, scratches developed into major infections, Indians killed a share, others started too late in life, some froze to death, some starved. But more survived. And California filled like a boomtown.[77]

The philosophy of the cowboy is not spoken, but tacit. It must remain what he was, not what he said.[78]

This then, is the impact of the West. A beacon to the world illuminating the belief that progress is accidental and miraculous and unplanned. . . . The West has given the nation a faith in unplanned progress. Despite the heady pleasure of an occasional bonanza, this impact is not an unmixed blessing.[79]

To argue which facets of the frontier experience have outlived their utility can be argued interminably, but certainly the wistful look backwards which Americans, informed and uninformed, cast toward the violence associated with the frontier has no place in a nation whose frontier has worn away. The time for everyone, from scenario writers to political breast beaters to economic and social individualists, to proclaim the virtues of the frontiersman and his reliance on simple solutions and direct action does not befit a nation whose problems are corporate, community, and complex.[80]

But the Driskill [Hotel in Austin] was always memorable. Like the difference between a gown and a dress, the Driskill has taken time to be courturiered, to be created and tailored, rather than just sewed and hemmed and put out to be worn.[81]

Scholars are sometimes accused of biting the hand that feeds them. If they possess the integrity they are supposed to, they will do just that. Every institution and person needs to be nipped at now and then.[82]

Academics everywhere are generally as rigid as rednecks, as conservative as successful farmers, and as irrational as zealots.[83]

In some ways The University of Texas at Austin reminds one of those gentle giants you occasionally run into—big enough and muscular enough to bully its arrogant way throughout the neighborhood, but electing instead to disguise its strength and downplay its successes.[84]

In my own instance, I have been tempted a number of times to leave the University of Texas, but the question always rises—do you abandon it to the rascals?[85]

He [folklorist J. Frank Dobie] belonged to the campfire and a ring of silence, where a man lets his words and thoughts lie on the wind awhile before moving on to the next stanza.[86]

If this little tribute sounds as if I am in love with Nettie Lee Benson [archivist of the University of Texas Latin American Collection], that's the way it is supposed to read. Forty years in and out of her presence has marked me, seduced me, even uplifted an unwilling sinner like me . . . Lord, what a privilege to have lived in the same environment with her![87]

It's a difficult world into which you're [Joseph McComb] being born, but that adds to the zest. When you get discouraged remember that every time a baby is born, the human race gets another chance. I'm glad you are here to give me that chance.[88]

Youth has little to do with the young. In fact, youth is not a time of life, youth is a state of mind. . . . When you [honor students] get down to basics, the world of ideas has no boundaries, no fences, no horizons. It is a world in which the imagination can soar, in which good talk can wander in any direction, in which minds can meet and clash and give off sparks—not sparks of heat, but sparks of light. You haven't played it safe with gentlemanly "C's." Don't play it safe in the years ahead. Instead honor yourselves and your school by inviting the kind of trouble that transforms education and life itself into an unending sequence of adventures.[89]

The Bible starts with Genesis and reaches an emotional, if not logical, conclusion with Revelations. Not Owen Ulph. He starts nowhere [in his book, *The Fiddleback*], moves forward and backward, sometimes simultaneously, spreads prose across the pages like greasewood across alkaline Western deserts, and scatters explosions of brilliance and insight like bombs detonating an ammunition dump. The effect is sometimes breathtaking . . . Ulph [writes] with the earthiness and utility of a pasture dark with dried cow chips.[90]

True, we [the Texas State Historical Association] will always be hedged in by interior linemen known as Time, Money, and Personnel, but each of these opponents can be blocked out of the play through perserverance and shrewd promotion.[91]

We [historians for a national foundation for the social sciences] believe that through the study of mankind and the social being, we really get a second look at ourselves which not only gives us the grand opportunity to live twice, but also the sometime opportunity to do something constructive about that life.[92]

Being a historian has certain similarities to running a house of prostitution—no mater how often you sell the product of the house, the product remains in as plentiful supply as when the first sale was made. History is self-replacing. There is always more to be done, and there are always new interpretations.[93]

Much of Frantz's writing, particularly articles, came from his speeches, and the cadence of his words often reveals that they were meant to be spoken. He relished the chance to make a speech, to tell his stories, to create laughter, to exercise his mind, and to give his audience something to think about. He enjoyed public adulation, wanted people to like him, and spoke often—to business groups, academics, students, University of Texas alumni, historical groups, and community gatherings. It was through these frequent public speeches that Joe became widely known and very popular. During the United States Bicentennial in 1976 when he was a member of the state organizing board, he spoke at a rate of about once per week. It is reasonable to think that a lot more people have heard him speak than have read his writings.

Topics for speeches expanded with time and he spoke with variations about the University of Texas, cowboys, the frontier, Texas Independence, Walter Prescott Webb, the importance of libraries, John F. Kennedy, Lyndon B. Johnson, national parks, and oral history. A talk about the "Frontier Reexamined" he gave seventeen times, and he spoke to UT alumni groups about the importance of higher education almost every year on March 2, Texas Independence Day, for at least twenty years.[94] At Schulenberg High School he lost his voice in the midst of an evening commencement address.[95] In Mexico or South America he would try to speak with his "home-grown" Spanish, and after one such event a listener commented, "That's the first historical address I've ever heard given in the present tense."[96]

Frantz drew upon his large repertoire of anecdotes, mixed them as necessary, elaborated, rambled a bit, sometimes spoke with little preparation, usually left people something to chew on, and was always entertaining. Once, Al Lowman scheduled him to speak to the Westerners in San Antonio and since Frantz procrastinated in sending a topic for his talk, Lowman made one up—"Sin in Parker County, 1935–1939." That would teach him, by golly. Frantz came, spoke, and conquered. He left them "rolling in the aisles" and Lowman was left amazed and gratified.[97] In an apparent emergency situation he was asked to fill in for a missing speaker at a Texas Library Association meeting in 1967. Afterwards, Peck Westmoreland Jr., the editor of *Texas Libraries*, asked for a copy of the talk and Frantz replied:

> Dear Peck. The trouble with sending you a copy of my speech is that I had exactly five little cryptic words to guide me. The writing of the speech took place during the period between the conclusion of lunch and the setting up of chairs in the next room. You couldn't make much of that, even if I could find it.[98]

With his nasal, Texas accent, and puckish wit Frantz gained a reputation as a "folksy, down-home tale-spinner."[99] His talks often began with some funny self-effacing statement. In a luncheon address to the West Texas Historical Association in 1964 he said, "For an ordinary historian—and I do presume to be at least ordinary—to come before a group of West Texas historians to talk about books is tantamount to my coming off the sandlot to teach Willie Mays the secrets of baseball. In neither case is there likely to be any glory for me, or profit for you."[100]

Typical was his beginning comment at the conference, "Texas in Transition," in 1986. Frantz had become a de facto historian for the Lyndon Johnson White House by this time, and he knew the family well. He related that he once shared a taxi with Luci Johnson in New York to travel from LaGuardia Airport to downtown. The cab driver recognized Luci and talked and talked to her all the way to her hotel. After letting her off, the driver turned to Frantz to find out where he was going, and asked, "You're not anybody important are you?" "Since then," Frantz concluded, "I've known where I stood."[101] This was the Frantzian equivalent of Walter Webb's Gunter-Hotel cure for pompousness.

His speeches led Frantz in a roundabout way to the most impor-

Frantz signs *Texas: A Bicentennial History* in a state ceremony. He put the volume together in six weeks. He sat on the floor surrounded by reference books and dictated into a tape recorder. The manuscript was transcribed by Ruth Mathews, and revised by Judith Austin of the Idaho State Historical Society. Governor William P. Hobby Jr. (center) and State Librarian Dorman H. Winfrey (right) stand behind him. *Photograph from Joe B. Frantz Papers, Center for American History, University of Texas at Austin. CN 10790.*

tant academic accomplishment of his career, the Lyndon B. Johnson Oral History Project. Late in 1963 he gave a speech, "The American West—Child of Federal Subsidy," to the luncheon meeting of Phi Alpha Theta, the history student honorary society, at the American Historical Association convention in Philadelphia. His point was that the heralded independence of the West was a myth, and his phrase,

"The truth is that from start to finish he was subsidized from his brogans to his sombrero," was quoted in newspapers from the *Washington Post* to the *San Francisco Chronicle*.[102] This brought him to the attention of Stewart Udall, the secretary of interior, and an appointment to the Advisory Board on National Parks, Monuments, and Historic Sites in 1964.[103] For Joe B. it was a choice appointment because he was funded to visit every national park in the nation. He loved it. It was a wonderful way to travel, and he eventually became vice chairman of the board.

In April 1966 in order to publicize the opening of Big Bend National Park, Lady Bird Johnson with an entourage of reporters took a float trip on the Rio Grande. Joe Frantz, soon to be director of the Texas State Historical Association, was included, along with Cactus Pryor, to help provide campfire entertainment. There was also an Odessa chuck wagon and music from Sul Ross College. Pryor, who impersonated a prospector, quipped, "If I want to do any talking I just talk to my jackass. I understand in Washington it's just the opposite." Lady Bird laughed. Frantz quoted a cowboy description of Big Bend: "You go south from Fort Davis until you come to the place where rainbows wait for rain, and the big river is kept in a stone box, and water runs uphill. And the mountains float in the air, except at night when they go away to play with other mountains." He said, "So we sit here tonight—in a forbidding land amidst friendly people." It was a successful venture and afterwards Frantz sent everyone copies of his snapshots.[104] Most importantly, the Big Bend trip brought Joe into close friendship with Lady Bird. Afterwards, a warm correspondence flourished between them.[105]

Joe had been fishing in political waters for awhile. He was a dedicated Democrat, and offered his services to the Kennedy administration through Arthur M. Schlesinger Jr., while commenting, "I have never been able to drum up any enthusiasm for Lyndon Johnson, admiring him for his wiliness more than anything else and realizing

In 1968 Frantz met with President Lyndon Johnson to discuss a program to document the administration through interviews. LBJ was careful about the selection of the director and finally endorsed Frantz by simply introducing him to others as the man running his oral history project. *Photograph by Jack Kightlinger; courtesy LBJ Library, Austin, Texas.*

the advantage he has of operating without principle."[106] Schlesinger was noncommittal. Frantz wrote again offering his help, and noted that several times a year someone mistook him for Schlesinger. "We must have a faint resemblance, but don't let that make you gloomy," Frantz said, with no compliment to either of them.[107]

Joe congratulated President Lyndon Johnson on his election victory in 1964, and later urged him to appoint a historian in residence. He offered to make recommendations.[108] Frantz also asked Johnson for an appointment as ambassador to Ecuador based upon his academic trips to Chile, Peru, and Mexico.[109] These suggestions were not taken, but as trust between the two men grew Frantz became an informal historical advisor for the Johnson administration. LBJ had been scorched by Eric Goldman, an early historian in residence, and was understandably cautious. Nonetheless, Johnson ap-

The oral history team met with President and Mrs. Johnson in the Cabinet Room of the White House in September 1968 to start work. Johnson endorsed the program and promised not to intrude. Mrs. Johnson, however, aided by supplying names and helping to persuade some recalcitrant people to cooperate with the project. *Photograph by Yoichi Okamoto; courtesy LBJ Library, Austin, Texas.*

pointed Frantz to the National Historical Publications Commission in 1966 and to the Historical Advisory Committee of the National Aeronautics and Space Administration in 1968.[110]

As time began to run out for the Johnson administration there emerged internal advice about the merits of an oral history program to supplement the Johnson records. The idea of such a program to document the decisions of the administration with interviews had been around since 1964.[111] There had also been a disorganized scramble of interviews following the death of President Kennedy, and, moreover, the idea of tape-recorded memoirs about historical events was well established. The Columbia University project, started by Allen Nevins shortly after World War II, was widely known by historians. Johnson, who had always spent much of his time negotiating

The LBJ Oral History Project interviewed friends as well as enemies of Lyndon Johnson. Most people understood the historical significance of the effort and they were permitted to restrict the use of the material as they wished. The interviews became a part of the Lyndon Baines Johnson Presidential Library in Austin, and have become a primary source of information for anyone writing about the life and times of President Johnson. *Photograph from Joe B. Frantz Papers, Center for American History, University of Texas at Austin. CN 10789.*

by telephone, readily understood the need for oral history to recapture with interviews such ephemeral information. Still, he was very cautious about who would record his accomplishments. For the president this was a difficult time of war, protests, and public criticism.

In 1967 Herman Kahn, the assistant archivist for presidential libraries, provided a report to the administration about oral history, outlining the high cost, the need for professional standards, and its usefulness for the future.

Despite the expense of oral history, when properly accomplished it produces unique material, the value of which can hardly be measured in terms of monetary cost. Most important is the fact that the evidence which it captures and preserves is perishable, for it will disappear from the memories of those who have it if it is not retrieved and preserved while they still can recall those facts which exist only in their memories.

For this reason it is suggested that it is not too early to initiate an oral history program covering the life and career of President Lyndon Baines Johnson. . . .[112]

Frantz was asked by the administration to consult on this idea and he put together a proposal. At first the presidential advisors thought the program could be carried out by a young Ph.D., but they shortly changed their minds to recommend a larger project with an established historian as director. Although several major historians were considered, Frantz was the natural choice since the Johnson Presidential Library was to be located on the campus of the University of Texas, and because Frantz was sympathetic to Johnson. Douglass Cater, a senior advisor, met with Frantz in May 1968 and was impressed. "I like the looks of the man," Cater told the president. "With your approval, I think we should move ahead at full speed to have a master plan ready for your review by the weekend. You may wish to tell him how important you believe this job is and to express appreciation for his willingness to drop everything and pitch in."[113]

Frantz shortly met with Johnson, dropped his summer and fall classes with the approval of the university, set up an advisory board of scholars, and proceeded to hire a team of young Ph.D.'s as interviewers. Johnson never asked Joe to do the work, he simply began to introduce the Texas historian with, "This is Joe Frantz. He's going to run my oral history project."[114] Funds for the program came from undisclosed, but private sources that were channeled through the University of Texas. Consequently, the oral history staff—Joe B. Frantz, Colleen T. Kain, Ruth Mathews, Mary Dale Ellis, T. Harrison Baker, Paige Mulhollon, David McComb, Steve Goodell, and Dorothy Pierce—met with President and Mrs. Johnson in the Cabinet

Room of the White House in September 1968. Johnson charged the group with finding out what had gone on with friends and enemies, and promised that he would respect the confidentiality of the interviews.[115]

The team systematically acquired a list of people to talk to, wrote letters of introduction, sent interviewers to various parts of the nation, and accumulated some five hundred memoirs in the first year. The secretarial staff transcribed the tapes; staff members gave them a light editing for grammar; the interviewees reviewed the transcripts and signed legal releases or restrictions; and the Johnson Library in Austin eventually took control of the collection. Most of the team went on to academic jobs after the first year, but Frantz remained as director until 1974, when the entire project was taken over by Michael Gillette of the LBJ Library. About seven hundred interviews had been conducted by that time.

"What I think I've achieved more than anything else is great anecdotal depth. And while most historians disdain anecdotes, some of them are quite revealing," Frantz concluded. "I think these tapes are important because they will emphasize the fact that the government is made up of people, with their foibles, strengths and weaknesses."[116] It was a project ideal for Joe B. Frantz. He had a satisfactory budget, secretarial staff, and travel money. He was able to talk to people at the highest reaches of government and society, and was able to add to his anecdotal storehouse. Thereafter, many of his speeches and publications involved the Johnson administration, or involved Frantz's position as one of the preeminent oral historians of the United States.

Most importantly, the oral history project provided an additional historical resource for future researchers. Oral histories are unusual among records of the past in that historians themselves ask the questions and seek the answers that, hopefully, the future will want to know about. Current historians are thus able to shape the writing of history in the future. Think how valuable it would be today if a historian had met with Abraham Lincoln to tape record questions and answers. Frantz accomplished this with the Johnson administration, one of the most tumultuous in American history.

Frantz's great legacy as a historian, therefore, is not with his popular speeches—they are ephemeral and will die with the memories of a generation of listeners. Who speaks now of Frantz as a great orator? Who remembers what he said? Some older people, perhaps, not many. The legacy is not with his writing—there is already revision with the "New Western History," and his publications linger only in bibliographies. The written words are fading, and only three books— *American Cowboy, Aspects of the American West,* and *6,000 Miles of Fence*—remain in print. Who quotes Frantz as they do Webb? But the oral history project is so important that it cannot be ignored by any serious scholar working on the Lyndon Johnson era. In the reading room on the eighth floor of the LBJ Library, at the side and behind the reference desk are a series of wooden files housing the transcripts of the interviews. The oral history interviews are used so much, about two thousand times a year, that they are kept readily at hand. Those interviews are Frantz's great legacy to scholarship.

With the completion of the oral history project Frantz neared the summit of his career. Everything came together for him in the middle of the 1970s when he was nationally recognized as a western, Texas, and oral history scholar. He wrote *Texas: A Bicentennial History,* which was published as a part of The States and The Nation series sponsored by the American Association for State and Local History. It was his kind of book. The general editor, James Morton Smith, said, "We have asked each author for a summing up—interpretive, sensitive, thoughtful, individual, even personal—of what seems significant about his or her state's history."[117]

Frantz was overcommitted, as usual, and due to be at the University of Maine for summer teaching in mid-1975, but the book

In 1977 some 450 people gathered at Webb's Friday Mountain Ranch to honor Frantz's accomplishments. He had just been appointed to the Webb Chair of History and Ideas at the University of Texas at Austin. *Photograph courtesy of News and Information Service, University of Texas at Austin.*

project paid him ten thousand dollars. He put it together in about six weeks before going to Maine—by sitting on the floor, circled by reference books, and talking into a tape recorder. Ruth Mathews, an oral history secretary, transcribed the dictation and gave him the manuscript to edit. Judith Austin of the Idaho State Historical Society provided further editing for the AASLH and reduced it to a fairly traditional, spare volume that conformed to the requirements of the series. Frantz did not object to the pruning and recalled Webb's advice to him from an earlier time, "You may do anything. But you ought to learn that you can't do everything." Frantz reflected, "I haven't learned."[118]

He was director of the Texas State Historical Association, 1966–1977; Southern Historical Association president, 1977–1978; Western History Association president, 1978–1979; a commissioner for the American Revolution Bicentennial Commission of Texas appointed by the governor, 1975–1977; on the advisory board of the Na-

At the 1977 gathering to honor Joe Frantz at Webb's Friday Mountain Ranch, Ernest Wallace, president of the Texas State Historical Association, presented Frantz with an honorary life membership in the association. *Photograph courtesy of News and Information Service, University of Texas at Austin.*

tional Park Service, 1970–1984; and full professor of history at the University of Texas at Austin, 1959–1981. There were many other boards, commissions, committees, and advisory panels to which he belonged—enough to fill two, single-spaced, typewritten, letter-sized pages on a vita—but there was a price to pay.

Joe responded in 1974 to C. B. Smith Sr., Webb's wealthy, Austin admirer, who wanted to know about a promised publication from the Webb Symposium: "If you can find some way of relieving me of the burdens of having lived too long in Austin and in Texas, so that the calls come from every level and every direction, then you would find me the most grateful person in the world."[119] Frantz said that he was working sixteen-hour days and that the symposium had been both a "delight and drudgery" because of the overload. Smith found a way. He provided half a million dollars to fund a Walter Prescott Webb Chair of History and Ideas, and asked the university to match it. This would supply about fifty thousand dollars a year to relieve a faculty member of classroom and administrative duties.[120]

Without much debate, in 1977 the University of Texas and the history department named Frantz to be the first holder of the Webb Chair, and in the same year he resigned as director of the Texas State Historical Association. He broke a tie vote in a council meeting to allow his assistant director, L. Tuffly Ellis, to take over, and summed up his feelings in a final address to the TSHA at its annual convention, "After all, life comes always from within, never from without. And inside me is nearly sixty years of watching and thinking and keeping quiet and turning over in my mind, and I want to share this while I have time."[121]

In the fall, at Webb's Friday Mountain Ranch, 450 people gathered for barbeque to honor Joe's accomplishments and new status. Present were the important elite of Texas such as John Tower, Ralph Yarborough, Darrell Royal, and Liz Carpenter. Floyd Tillman provided music and Frantz quipped, "It's like old home week—we used to have funerals like this in Weatherford." Joe was given a life membership in the Texas State Historical Association and a sketch of Friday Mountain by artist José Cisneros. "You must have been out of your minds to have come this far," he told the guests, "but I love the irrationalities in people."[122] It was a golden moment for the orphan from Weatherford, who wanted approval and friendship from all he met. People loved him and he loved people; it was the grand triumph of a lifetime.

ENDGAME

The construction of human tragedy involves choices; the drama of tragedy invokes pathos; the portrayal of tragedy demonstrates imperfections; the conclusion of tragedy is ruination. Some readers will view the last sixteen years of Joe B. Frantz's travels as tragic, because his academic career unraveled through his own decisions, and because the mantle of Texas history inherited from Webb was left in tatters. Starting at age sixty he experienced three divorces involving four wives, two beloved daughters, three stepchildren, and five grandchildren. These divisions created outrage, sustained anger, confusion, loss of friends, bitterness, and public humiliation. No one on the outside can ever measure or express the extent of pain in these divorces. Perhaps, the daughters' statement read by son-in-law Scott Fleming at the memorial service says enough: "He made some choices and decisions that were inconsistent and incomprehensible with the father we knew."[1]

Frantz ended life in financial debt. His fortune was almost gone by the end of the second marriage, he could work only half-time, and for three years during the mid-1980s he neglected to pay his income taxes. Everyday bills remained unpaid after the Internal Revenue Service moved in on his wages and left him only seventy-five dollars a week to live on. His surviving wife, Betsy Chadderdon Frantz, transferred his Corpus Christi home to the IRS in order to settle accounts with the federal government.[2]

He had always been somewhat inept and lax about debt payment, but in August 1988 he composed a letter "To All my Creditors" about his "year of the locusts." "I will pay you as I work this out. I WILL PAY YOU. You will be glad to have me as a customer. Meanwhile you will collect interest on my account."[3] He wrote to the First Union Mortgage Corporation in Raleigh, North Carolina, about a threatened foreclosure on his house, "I am nearly 72 years old, and would like to die in the house, rundown and dated though it may be. (It reminds me of me, I might add)." And, "Do you want me to join the homeless? Corpus Christi is warmer than Raleigh . . . but it gets cold and rainy, and bridges to sleep under are few."[4] He was ill with diabetes and eyesight and heart troubles that often went untreated, in part at least, through his own negligence. When he discovered his name removed from *Who's Who in America* in 1991 he railed, "Am I dead, and not willing to admit it? Have I gone downhill and am less than I was? Are you blaming me for the Cubs' failure to perform this season?"[5]

Does all of this add up to tragedy? Perhaps, but it depends on your point of view. "Tragedy," noted Ralph Waldo Emerson in 1844, "is in the eye of the observer, and not in the heart of the sufferer."[6] This would seem to be the case with Joe B. Frantz. He did have problems, but he never gave up on life. He remained cheerful, puckish, and ebullient. His sense of humor never deserted him. His engagement with others did not erode in corrosive self-pity. He tried to explain circumstances to his wounded loved ones, but he did not blame anyone but himself for his decisions, nor curse his fate. Exercising his God-given talent, he continued to speak and teach until physically unable. He recognized that he had but a brief moment of time on earth, and reached to embrace all he could while he could. Did this amount to tragedy? Not from his point of view. Life was a grand adventure, a glorious journey, a blessing.

While lecturing on the *Delta Queen* in 1978 he met Anne Maschka—twenty-eight years old, bright, attractive, married, with aspirations to be a writer. They fell in love and both divorced their spouses so they could marry each other. The divorces were final in 1980, and meanwhile they lived openly together. Although a young unmarried couple living together is a common event at the present time, to the older generation in Austin and elsewhere in 1978 it was a scandal. This event coincided with Joe's presidencies of the Southern Historical Association and the Western Historical Association, and, as might be expected, the gossip swirled through the associations as Frantz broke with his first family and his Weatherford relatives.

In December 1978 he took Anne with him to a meeting of the Philosophical Society of Texas, a staid, mature group that would be certain to "harrumph," and did. Joe asserted that "my living with Anne has been the one honest, forward, redemptive step of my life."[7] Terrell Webb warned, "You aren't getting too much sympathy," and commented, "If you have to have this woman, then have her. But don't be so damn honest about it!"[8] He was called in by Dean Robert D. King and warned that his personal life might cost him the Webb Chair, and an inside friend tipped him that the regents were mad as "Dobermans" over his "live-in" situation.[9] Although it is impossible to measure the effect of this agitation about his marital situation, it certainly colored the background of his remaining years in Austin.

At the end of the spring semester 1979 Joe and Anne left Austin for Europe, where he had an assignment from the Fulbright Commission to set up an American Studies program in Budapest, Hungary. The timing was bad. He was not feeling well, suffering from angina and breathlessness. Also, he left it to his teaching assistant to complete the last two weeks of class, give the final exam, and assign term grades. Although this sort of abandonment might have happened before at the University of Texas, for most professors such behavior would be considered a violation of responsibility, if not of contract. While in Greece he checked back with the department and was read a letter from President Lorene Rogers:

> Dear Joe. For a number of weeks I have been holding on my desk a letter from Dean Robert D. King which recommends that you be replaced as holder of the Webb Chair of History and Ideas in the Department of History as of Sept. 1, 1979. I have given long and serious consideration to this matter, and as much as I regret to have to take this action, I feel I must act affirmatively on the recommendation which has come to me.[10]

The letter went on to state that he could return to the department as a tenured professor of history. There was no explanation in the message, however, for her action. Frantz rushed home and after delay met with President Rogers and Dean King. The meeting was worse than fruitless, because Rogers also removed Frantz from an authorized history of the university which he had drafted with the help of Margaret Berry, a University of Texas administrator. Rogers said about the manuscript, "You have managed to insult every group connected with the university—the regents, the administration, the faculty, the students, the legislature, and the alumni."[11]

With questions left unanswered, the day after the meeting Frantz entered Seton Hospital in Austin for a triple-bypass heart operation. Through the summer he had a bitter fight with his department chairman over sick-leave pay, and in August, again with no explanation, Rogers restored him to the Webb Chair. There was an agreement, however, that he would resign the chair in June 1981, one year short of its five-year term, and that he would receive university funds for a Fulbright lecture series to Italy for 1980–1981.[12]

While in Italy he gave talks, toured, and wrote minor commentaries on the 1980 presidential election for the *Texas Observer*, and on lust and the Pope for *Playboy* magazine.[13] Anne taught English at the Center for American Studies in Rome to help meet expenses.[14]

His sentiments toward the university, meanwhile, soured and he wrote to an academic friend, Frank Vandiver:

> Now, I could make a tedious recital of all of this [problems at the university]. But it gives you an idea of why I have decided that I am spending more time fighting the system than I am doing what I want and need to do: write all those things I have been storing up for years while I chased goat feathers for the University. I am cutting my ties and getting out.[15]

On May 31, 1981, he officially retired from the history department, though he would continue to teach half-time, and on August 31, 1981, he officially resigned from the Webb Chair. Unofficially, his relationship with the University of Texas had ended. There were no more committee assignments, no special duties for the university, no call for speeches, and few invitations.

With all of these complications it is easy to understand why he missed publication deadlines and research opportunities. He misplaced a book he was supposed to review for the *Florida Historical Quarterly*; he was late with an evaluation of a book manuscript for the University of Texas Press; he failed to write a chapter on Hobart Taylor for a book on black Texas leaders; and he missed sending an article to the American Folklife Center. "'Belated' seems to be my middle name," he said, "unless it is 'benighted.'"[16] He lost an opportunity to obtain a contract for a book on Moses Austin, and because of conflict with the owners failed, after extensive research and writing, with a publication of a history of the YO Ranch near Kerrville.[17] He also lost the chance, through his inaction, to edit an oral history account of the Johnson administration. I had prepared a rough draft for joint authorship, and Frantz had contacted publishers about a book.[18] Meanwhile, Merle Miller ransacked Frantz's oral history work at the LBJ Library and put together *Lyndon: An Oral Biography*. The book briefly made it to the bottom of the *New York Times* best-seller list.[19]

Frantz, however, did manage to publish *The Forty-Acre Follies:*

This photograph appeared on the back of the dustjacket for *The Forty-Acre Follies*, which Frantz wrote in the early 1980s. The book, a critique of the University of Texas, was written during difficult times of health, divorce, and work. This is one of the few adult pictures of Frantz without glasses. *Photograph from Joe B. Frantz Papers, Center for American History, University of Texas at Austin. CN 10792.*

An Opinionated History of the University of Texas. Lorene Rogers had removed him from work on the official history of the university, and Frantz appealed to the new president, Peter T. Flawn, when he replaced her. Flawn flatly dismissed his efforts to help, placed Berry in charge of the project, and told Frantz that he could do whatever he wished with his personal notes and manuscript. Frantz revised and extended the manuscript to fourteen hundred pages, and sent it to Texas Monthly Press with the biting acknowledgment: "I should also thank Governor Shivers, Ambassador Clark, Lorene Rogers, and Peter Flawn, without whose discouragement or challenge I would probably still be contemplating this volume twenty years from now. . . . They provided the indignation I needed to be spurred into action."[20]

Texas Monthly cut the manuscript in half and softened his rhetoric. "I was planning to make everyone hate me," Frantz wrote to a friend, "except those few who would shout 'hallelujah!' at last the truth."[21] The book, nonetheless, was well received by regional reviewers, and won the Southwestern Booksellers Association award for the best nonfiction Texas book of the year. Kent Biffle of the *Dallas Morning News* summed up the reactions: "This history is irreverent, almost disrespectful at times, but at others sentimental."[22]

It was more of a memoir, however, than a history. There were no footnotes, no index, and poor chronological balance. He sympathized with the integration of minorities, and said little about the Vietnam War on campus—obviously, he stood by Lyndon Johnson on that issue. The chapters on athletics are pure Frantzian, filled with zest, and revealing a path not taken. He could have been a giant among sports writers. He criticized most administrators, some professors, but few students. Most importantly, he explained the importance of universities and learning and teaching.

Here . . . is where students learn to be critical, to turn over rocks, to examine evidence, to take no one at his word. They can challenge the professor and get away with it as they never could at home, as they seldom will later on in business. They can cast stones at sacred cows and posit new theories and ideas with all the seriousness of a Kant or a Kafka. They don't have to be team players. They can, in short, learn to think on their own.

This university should be first of all a disorderly place where fifty thousand people more or less the same age believe that the world can still be saved. Since soon enough they will find out that the world doesn't want to be saved, they should be permitted those four to six years of illusion while they are here. They will also learn soon enough that the world is a place fenced in by rules and conventions and channels, most of them negative and progress-inhibiting. And so they should approach their university years as a period when they can seek to relieve the oppressions of unnatural rules and conventions while building their own sets of values.

A university should be a place where the shades are raised and the world beyond is revealed, with no attempt to control the view.

For all its faults and its interrupted rhythms, I still think college is the best place for any halfway intelligent person between the ages of eighteen and twenty-five to be.[23]

The Forty-Acre Follies was Joe B. Frantz's valedictory to the institution that had educated him, nurtured him, honored him, and given him room to grow. He thought that the institution would be, like himself, mature enough to withstand without rancor the exposure of faults. It wasn't. Although he was still on campus and teaching part-time in the history department, the man who was "Mr. Texas" in 1977 was not invited to participate in the centennial celebration of his university in 1983. The university, for example, started an oral history project as a part of its commemoration, but Frantz, one of the foremost oral historians in the nation, was not given a role. It was time for him to leave.

Joe had been fruitlessly searching for another job since 1979—at Southern Methodist University, at the Huntington Library in California, as a correspondent for the *Los Angeles Times* in Chile, and as the historian of the House of Representatives in Washington, D.C.[24] To his good fortune he was passing through Garrison Hall when a phone call came to the department from Pat Carroll of Corpus

Christi State University, asking for someone to help with the 1984 summer school teaching. It was thus that Carroll, who had received a Ph.D. in Latin American history at the University of Texas, spoke to Frantz, whom he did not know, and requested a graduate student to teach U.S. and Texas history courses. Joe said he would scout about.[25]

A few days later Joe called back and said that he had good and bad news. The bad news was that no graduate students could come, and the good news, or bad news as the case might be, was that Joe would like to come. How much was the pay? Carroll paused, checked with the dean, and called back. "I have good and bad news," he told Joe. "The bad news is that the university will not pay the rate for a Ph.D.," he said, and there was silence on the other end of the line. "The good news is that they will pay you twice that much." Joe replied, "I think that I will like it there." When Carroll informed him that there would also be a per diem allotment, Frantz said, "I think that I will let you be my full-time negotiator."[26]

Joe B. taught in Corpus Christi for six weeks, returned to teach the following spring, and then remained on the coast. His marriage with Anne broke up late in 1983, followed by divorce in 1984–1985. CCSU provided a warm refuge for Joe and the university awarded him the Margaret and Paul Turnbull Professorship which gave him a half-time salary and per diem to teach two courses a semester— American Business Enterprise, and Texas in the Twentieth Century. President Alan Sugg told him, "If you will come, you will be free of all age restrictions and can hold the chair until the day that I have to come to school and show you which way to face the class."[27] So, Joe left Austin and made his home in Corpus Christi.

Frantz resigned from the University of Texas at Austin on January 16, 1986, and the following March the department hosted a farewell party for him at Saengerrunde Hall next to Scholz Beer Garden, the legendary watering hole in Austin for students and faculty. Dean

Robert King, who remained a friend in spite of all difficulties, announced, "I can't think of anybody over the years that I have liked as much as Joe Frantz. He's earthy, and he has known everybody in the state. And he has always been solid and sensible and decent. Joe is one of my heroes."[28] Everyone there—with perhaps the exception of his soon-to-be-divorced third wife—toasted his good health and wished him good luck.

Joe found Corpus Christi interesting and he plunged into the life of the city and the university without hesitation and with his usual enthusiasm. He joined the Westside Business Association, a group of some sixty Hispanic business people who met every Thursday morning for breakfast. Usually, they invited a speaker, and they tried to make Corpus Christi a better community. It was reminiscent of the Headliner's Club which Frantz had helped establish in Austin many years before. The business association raised the money to erect a statue of Blas María de la Garza Falcón for the waterfront boulevard in 1992.[29] Chiseled on the back of the pedestal are the names of the leaders of the association, all Hispanic with the exception of Joe B. Frantz. The list tells a quiet story amidst the swirling noisiness of the bayside traffic, the story of an aging scholar with no prejudices still interested in business matters, and an ethnic group acceptive of an outsider willing to join with them to celebrate the heritage of the city. It marks in stone a small triumph of open-mindedness in a city, state, and nation that requires tolerance for survival.

Joe also joined in the effort to list Corpus Christi as a port of call for the replica ships of Christopher Columbus, sailing from Spain during the Quincentennial in 1992. He became involved with the city's Quincentenary Committee and was chair of the Historical Subcommittee. With others he made four trips to Spain, trips that resulted not only in a visit by "Las Carabelas" to Corpus Christi as a port of call, but also in the selection of Corpus Christi as the permanent

After leaving the University of Texas at Austin for Corpus Christi State University Frantz continued writing and speaking. In 1986 he took part in the forum "Texas in Transition," hosted by the LBJ Library and the LBJ School of Public Affairs. "These are the times when we don't know where we're going, but we do get the feeling we're going somewhere else," he commented in the opening (Michael L. Gillette, ed., *Texas in Transition*, Austin: Lyndon Baines Johnson Library, Lyndon B. Johnson School of Public Affairs, 1986, p. 4). *Photograph courtesy of News and Information Service, University of Texas at Austin.*

berth for the replica ships in the United States.[30] Frantz played a background role, part of the chorus, so to speak, and he is not featured in the newspaper reports of the effort. Again, however, his name can be seen on the pedestal of the Columbus statue placed at the dock of the *Niña, Pinta,* and *Santa María.*

He dabbled and stirred in local politics and went to the Democratic Party county convention as a Jesse Jackson delegate in 1988.[31] He wrote an essay for the *Caller-Times* urging Governor William Clements to raise new taxes for state benefit, and aroused an indignant response from a citizen of nearby Rockport: "With Ed Harte, Jerry Norman and a few dozen other dreary left-wing advocates oozing their bilge onto the editorial pages of Corpus Christi's daily sheet, why spend the time and money dredging up the ex-TU [sic] resident, pro-welfare nincompoop to add to the swill?"[32] With a newfound liberal friend from the university, philosopher Jim McClellan, Frantz turned over the compost of local conservatism with a pitchfork editorial that examined the mean-spiritedness of U.S. relations with Cuba. This brought three months of irate letters to the editor and the offer of a one-way ticket to the communist island.[33] Frantz had often written to local newspapers, and he relished the educational value of controversy.

At Corpus Christi State University he found a comfortable home. The Baptist Church started the university in 1947 on Ward Island in a former radar installation of the U.S. Navy. Hurricane Celia scoured the area in 1970, and the connection with the church ended in 1971. Citizens of Corpus Christi purchased the land with a bond issue, gave it to the state, and the Texas legislature authorized a junior-senior branch of Texas A&I. With the aid of local funding the university rebuilt the campus with low, flat-roofed, rectangular, modern buildings on its spectacular site facing Corpus Christi Bay. As a part of Texas A&I it opened in 1973. It was called Corpus Christi State University from 1977 to 1989, when the legislature made it a part of

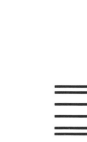

Thank you for choosing a Texas State Historical Association book. We hope you enjoy it. Please let us hear from you. Complete this postage-paid card and:

☐ Check here if you would like us to send you a complete catalogue of all TSHA publications.

☐ Check here if you would like information about membership in the Texas State Historical Association. Members receive a 15% discount on all TSHA publications.

Name _____

Address _____

City _____ State _____ Zip _____

Texas A&M and authorized freshman and sophomore classes. It was renamed Texas A&M University-Corpus Christi (TAMCC) in 1993, and lower-division classes began in 1994. The irony did not escape Joe B. who bought for Pat Carroll, a fellow longhorn now living in an Aggieland pasture, a University of Texas baseball cap made out of camouflage fabric.

The university competed for regional students with Texas A&I at Kingsville and Texas Southmost in Brownsville. The presence of Joe Frantz gave CCSU the prestige of a well-known major scholar, and he played the role of a senior statesman.[34] Speaking and writing, of course, continued.[35] Leaving the problems with the University of Texas behind in Austin, Frantz arrived in Corpus Christi with the ambition of writing books about Lyndon Johnson, Sam Houston, Ralph Yarborough, Walter P. Webb, and Hector Garcia. He never started on Yarborough, Webb, or Houston; and the closest he came to Hector Garcia, the Hispanic doctor and leader of Corpus Christi, was to offer help to Pat Carroll with "Felix Longoria's Wake." This was a book about Hispanic activism after World War II, but Frantz was unable to finish it before he became ill. Carroll continues with the manuscript.[36] Frantz signed a contract with Texas Christian University Press for a book about Johnson, accepted an advance payment, and was unable to finish. In a letter to the press in 1988 he said, "I have had a chapter completed in rough draft since the beginning of September [1987], but never seem able to get to it until after midnight, when I metamorphose into a poor typist."[37]

In 1986 Joe supplied a brief survey of Texas history for a series in *Texas Highways*, and completed *Lure of the Land* with Mike Cox, a journalist and book dealer. Using rare nineteenth-century county maps Cox and Frantz told the story of settlement and the land in Texas. They split the writing task between them, but the coordinator had to spur Joe into action. "Joe," she wrote, "Too much time has lapsed since I've heard from you. Send words! We are falling behind!

Write! Work! Now!"[38] An editor had to blend the writing styles of the authors, and Joe groused, "He has drained the naturalness from the manuscript until it reads like an academic exercise. It will please the academics, but it won't attract the casual reader who can afford the coffee table to put it on. Pedestrian, no zip no more, safe. But, so be it."[39] *Lure of the Land*, however, sold out and won the Fehrenbach Award of the Texas Historical Commission for the best book of the year. It was Joe's last book, and memorably, it was recognized with a major state award for excellence.

Meanwhile, Joe, talkative and friendly, blended into the faculty at Corpus Christi. "Down here," he wrote to Helen, "it is like belonging to a small-town church. You're noticed when you're absent, so that I've been to more faculty meetings in five years than I did in 40 years at UT."[40] There was a change in Joe B., however. Although still writing, teaching, and giving speeches, he slowed down—like a man in retirement, like a man who has little else to prove, like someone who has seen much and knows he has little to fear, like someone who has faced his mortality. He took time for colleagues, took time to build friendships, took time to be useful, took time to listen. He was patient. The driving competition with fellow historians had disappeared; it made no difference anymore. He was respected as a wise old man, and like a true sage he had no arrogance. He came to Corpus Christi with a certain peace with the world and with himself.

The men at all levels liked his graciousness and generosity, the absence of vindictiveness. Women warmed to his charm, flirtation, and interest. He was not threatening or intimidating to women, rather more like a puppy to be cuddled and mothered. Children also responded to his interest and friendship. When he first moved to Corpus Christi he stayed for a few days with Pat Carroll and his family, but Pat with good nature later commented that he was glad to see Joe move out. Joe B. had charmed all the females of his family and they were falling in love with him. Later, when Pat's parents both died in the same year, to ease the distress, Joe called him at 5:00 A.M. and said, "I hear you're an orphan. Don't worry, I just adopted you," and then hung up.[41] This abrupt, heartfelt message of concern cemented a father-son sort of relationship between the two scholars.

He developed, moreover, a close friendship with Jim McClellan, a philosophy teacher his age who had married a younger woman. They had a similar background, understood one another, and became friends who could tease each other without offense. It was a rare comradeship between noncompetitive equals. They traveled together, poked fun at the political conservatives together, and enjoyed the foibles of humanity.[42] With younger colleagues such as Robert Wooster and Alan Lessoff, Frantz played a mentoring role. He wrote letters of recommendation for Wooster, and led Lessoff, an eastern-trained, urban historian, into a greater appreciation of his surroundings.[43] He even wrote the words for a musical composition by colleague Lawrence Weiner called "Quest for Peace."[44]

The faculty at TAMCC came to appreciate, if not love, Joe B. Frantz. They knew about his personal problems, and endured the public ones. When he moved from Austin, for example, Joe had his papers shipped to the library at the university. They were stacked in the basement, some eighty boxes or so, and, somehow, Joe took two and a half years to move them. The archivist Tom Kreneck (whom Joe had recommended to the university), interpreted this as mulishness related to a simple lack of interest in physically handling the boxes.[45] But Frantz was also stubborn in other matters. Ross Purdy, acting as the chair of the division, often had to send him notes nagging for book orders for forthcoming classes. In 1989 Purdy wrote in frustration, "I'm told that Walter P. Webb never was late in turning in *his* book orders."[46]

The colleagues watched as Joe married Kristina Faber, an English teacher at CCSU, in 1985. It was a mismatch that, though it lasted about a year, foundered from the beginning.[47] She attended the retirement party for Joe in Austin in the spring of 1986, but departed before the reception ended. In 1988 Kristina, angry, left Corpus Christi to teach in Pennsylvania. In debt and ill with high blood pressure and incipient diabetes, Joe courted Betsy Chadderdon of Houston. Betsy, energetic and vivacious, directed student and alumni services at the University of Texas School of Public Health in Houston. They met and talked after speeches he had given, and she asked in 1989, "If you marry again, would you marry me?" He thought it over and in 1990 they began a long-distance marriage with Betsy in Houston and Joe visiting on weekends.[48]

In 1991 Joe began to suffer noticeable health problems. He composed but did not send a health memo to his colleagues, in which he admitted that he tilted a bit when he walked, suffered some memory loss, became confused at times, and was tired. "But, if I am failing or going to hell physically, I prefer to do so without comment," he concluded.[49] In 1992 his diabetes progressed quickly from pills to needles for control. He lost twenty-five pounds, had trouble walking, and suffered blurred vision.[50] He admitted to Helen, "I'm late and confused a good bit of the time these days."[51] His diabetes spun out of control in 1993 and he wrote a friend that most of the time from April to September was a blur.[52] There were stories and gossip about his physical decline—he could climb stairs only one at a time, he rambled in speeches, he hiked across a busy six-lane freeway, he walked into a column without seeing it, he began lecturing to the wrong class.

The president who had hired him said that Joe could stay until he had to be pointed in the direction of the class. This meant until such a time when he was so broken down that he could no longer meet the demands of teaching. That time had arrived, and Joe sent in a memo of resignation: "Reason: advanced age and the onset of the early springtime of my senility. Or, to put it in personal terms, I wish to leave before passersby bow to me and I hear them whisper to each other as they move on, 'When?'"[53] As his health broke, the school turned to Betsy. She along with Joe and associates finished his classes. Still, he presented the commencement address in August 1993.

> You commence to get educated, not in the classroom, but by your vocation, whether carpenter or corporate president. . . . The mind is an incredible machine, and its memory and power of synthesis can be equally incredible. Don't make snap judgements, but don't be afraid if your mind leaps out ahead of you. Breakthroughs emerge from such experiences.[54]

Betsy took him home with her to Houston to ease his passage through the fog. He lectured twice for a continuing-studies program for Rice University, but he could do no more. He traveled to Santa Fe to see his friend of a half-century, Gene Hollon, once again, and attended a Texas vs. Oklahoma football game for the last time. On October 13 Betsy took him to Hermann Hospital. His journey was over.

EPILOGUE

Probably anyone who writes a biography about someone they admire mourns the death at the end of the story. Frank Vandiver, a superb biographer of soldiers, told a group of us graduate students at Rice University in the early 1960s that he could hardly bear to kill his subject, Stonewall Jackson. He fretted, paced, and stared at his typewriter for a month before he was able to sit down and fire, again, the fatal bullet that killed the Civil War soldier a century earlier. So it is with me.

It is hard to bring to a close, again, the life of a man who had given so much of himself to me. When I joined the oral history team in Washington, D.C., in 1968 I was a person who was screwed down tight. That is, the kind of person who thought it was necessary to own only white, button-down, long-sleeved, oxford-cloth, dress shirts. After all, they would go with everything you needed to wear, even blue jeans, and you could roll up the sleeves in the summertime. The Chief and I lived together for six months in the Columbia Plaza apartments in the heart of the city, and he went to work on me to loosen the screws a bit.

He arranged for the team to take weekend excursions—to the Great Falls of the Potomac, to the hiking trails of the Smokies, to hear the music of Charlie Byrd, to see *The Man of La Mancha*, to visit the eastern shore of Maryland, to eat lobster at Bookbinder's in

Philadelphia, to try soft shell crabs at a coastal fishing shack, to go to an All-Star baseball game at RFK stadium, to stand on the cold, rainy sidewalks of Washington for the Eisenhower funeral caisson to pass, to witness the misty, solemn grandeur of Gettysburg. All the while he told me stories and anecdotes, such as Walter Prescott Webb's retort when a department chair asked what he had learned at a meeting of the American Historical Association: "Oh hell, Hanke, I took one look at the program and then went to see *Guys and Dolls* and *The Consul* and I don't know what else. I can listen to historians any time!"[1]

I asked the Chief if he ever took a vacation. Frantz pointed out that he took vacations along with his work. It was a totality for him, and people, he thought, should be aware of opportunities to take small excursions as they go along. He passed on other points of wisdom: a person could go around the world with a single credit card, book royalties should be counted only as pleasant surprises and not be expected for income, and a writer should never bother to reply to critics. Don't comment harshly about papers at conferences either, it is hard enough for young scholars to stand up and speak. Don't try to reform confirmed smokers, they have already heard your arguments and are self-righteous. Follow the credo of Lyndon Johnson: if you admit that you are tired, you're through. A study of train and air schedules is time well spent, you may have a sudden opportunity to travel. Take a lot of snapshots, they are the sparks of memory. Buy lunch for a student who has no money and then later, that successful student will buy lunch for another. Joe frequently paid a restaurant bill, or the cost of my ticket, and told me about the intergenerational generosity that had passed from Barker to Webb to himself.

He also teased a bit. In 1972 when I hosted a party for him after a February lecture at Colorado State University, a neighborhood Persian cat defiantly hopped up, squatted, and urinated on a tub of clean party ice on my back porch. I was furious (and still am), but

Frantz believed in taking side excursions from the path of work. During the Oral History Project he took time to hike the Smoky Mountains with David McComb, enjoy a baseball game with Dorothy Pierce, and hold his namesake, Joseph McComb. *From author's collection.*

the Chief roared and crooned, "Oh, thank heaven for Seven Eleven."[2] He enjoyed the misadventures of life and said that it was because I had not invited the cat to the party. With all of his patient work the screws loosened. I wrote to him in 1977 for his party at Friday Mountain:

I cannot attend your grand reception, but I have declared Joe B. Frantz day in Fort Collins, Colorado, put up a sign, turned on country-western music, and pulled on a Lone Star T-shirt. And it's in your honor. It's your fault too. Ten years ago I would have considered it silly to put up a sign, and a Lone Star T-shirt would have been a waste of money. After all, an efficient wardrobe needs only white shirts. Then you don't have to make a choice about what to wear every day. Back then I was not addicted to coffee either. Thanks a lot . . . hooked on a twenty-five-cents-a-day habit. I've since acquired a son named Joe, and an awareness of things such as the Dallas Cowboys and George Jones, that wasn't there before. My life is thus somewhat more cluttered, but immeasurably expanded.[3]

I was not the only beneficiary of his attention, generosity, and stretching; there were others, such as Ronnie Davis, Pat Carroll, and Michael Gillette. He took the time to make people feel special and dignified, in different ways and for different reasons, so they could be better than they were. Consider, for example, this letter from George Woolfolk, a contemporary African-American historian from Prairie View A&M:

The black scholar works in a milieu that is basically designed to defeat his efforts. . . . You may know that all the money for trips and research comes out of the "Woolfolk" foundation. I have not had a paid leave of absence in the entire time I have worked here. The system never says to you that you have done well. . . . Thanks again to the best friend a man has ever had. Without such outside encouragement I would have to throw in the towel and quit.[4]

Joe touched the hearts and minds of countless people. There are hundreds of Joe Frantz stories from people who knew him well, and also from casual acquaintances. No biography of Joe can ever be complete, just approximate, and we can all take a warning from his own writing experience. Six years after completing his book on Borden, a "definitive" study he thought, a high school teacher found two volumes of additional Borden papers. Together they went on a quest and found forty-eight more volumes, along with pictures and account books, in an old tack house. Frantz concluded that nothing is ever definitive.[5] Still, historians try to be as comprehensive as possible.

A number of people talked to me about Joe, shared their insight, and deserve recognition and gratitude—Jim and Dorothy McClellan, Robert Wooster, Pat Carroll, Tom Kreneck, Alan Lessoff and Mineke Reinders, Paul Hain, Al Lowman, L. Tuffly Ellis, Colleen Kain, Ronnie Davis, Helen Frantz, Lisa Frantz Dietz, Jolie Frantz Fleming, James M. Cotten, and Betsy Chadderdon Frantz. Another major source of information was the eighty-four boxes of the unorganized Frantz papers that are at the University of Texas. Katherine Adams and Sara Clark of the Center for American History gave me advice and access to these materials. As I was going through his letters and manuscripts I had the feeling that his ghost was looking over my shoulder, saying, "Look here at this! Pay attention to that!" It was almost as if he had expected me to pay a visit. Other points of information, in addition, came from the departmental and the presidential papers of the University of Texas at Austin, and the papers of the Texas State Historical Association. Director Ron Tyler, George Ward, and Evelyn Stehling opened the door for research at the association.*

The brilliance of a many-faceted person such as Joe Frantz was sometimes stunning, sometimes shaded and subtle, sometimes wasted. He was good of heart, and yet injured people he loved. He taught willing students how to live, and yet made many mistakes in

---

Faculty at Texas A&M University-Corpus Christi made the suggestion for the biography and the university provided financial support.

his own life. Nonetheless, he did not scowl at life, and his chuckle and his nasal, "I see," as he listened made people feel worthwhile, somehow bigger. This desire and ability to produce an inner glow of pride in others merits perhaps the highest accolade that can be given a human being. He was able to make people feel good about themselves. Those of us who were able to travel his path with him, and share his rainbow, even for a while, were indeed fortunate.

SELECTED READINGS

DOCTORAL STUDENTS

BOOKS BY JOE B. FRANTZ

After failing health forced him to forgo classes at Texas A&M-Corpus Christi Frantz moved to Houston. To the end of his days he retained his optimism, wit, and fascination with life. *Photograph courtesy of Betsy Chadderdon Frantz.*

SELECTED READINGS

To paraphrase, or to lift quotations from an article or book does damage to the totality of a writer's thought. It would seem simple justice in the biography of a wordsmith like Joe B. Frantz to allow him somewhere along the line to have not only the first and last word, but all the words in between. Thus, I have appended three items.

The first is a newspaper article about "Mr. Rabbit," a pet who was killed in vicious fashion by roving dogs. Two years after the publication of this small news article as Joe was checking out at a grocery store, a clerk looked at his name, and said, "Oh, you must be the person who wrote about 'Mr. Rabbit.'" Writing is a solitary business, and an author can never be certain if anyone is reading. Joe had an answer here.

The second article was a speech, actually a funeral address, given for his good friend, Richard T. Fleming, a retired executive from Texas Gulf Sulphur Corporation, who created the Ex-Students' Writing Collection at the University of Texas. Fleming cared passionately for books and his country. The address demonstrates how Frantz could translate feelings into words.

The third is an academic article about Lyndon Johnson which was originally Joe's presidential address at the Southern Historical Association meeting in St. Louis in 1978. It represents his best thinking about the president and demonstrates the historical use of oral history.

A Hard Death, Faced Alone: Quietly Doing His Own Thing, 'Mr. Rabbit' Gets Torn to Bits

By Joe Frantz
UT History Professor

He wasn't six feet tall like Elwood P. Dowd's Harvey. And he lacked that dissolute leer and swagger of the Playboy bunny.

Actually he had cost only $1.75 at Austin Feed and Ranch Supply, where the woman who sold the little grey furry ball told me she had no instructions beyond giving him a home and whatever love we could spare.

So we took him home in a box, played with him, watched him cavort and frolic, and held him close without trying to smother him. My younger daughter Lisa, not given to such sentiment usually, cooed to him over and over the teen-age hit of yesteryear:

> Chantilly lace
> Pretty face
> A pony tail hanging down
> A wiggle in your walk
> A giggle in your talk
> To make the world go 'round.

This first appeared in the *Austin Statesman*, May 18, 1973.

And he would flex his busy nose in reply, lift his chinchilla-colored body for an Olympic leap, and come back to be sung to again.

Of course, he outgrew the box in the house and would wander in the halls and bedrooms in the dark until you were fearful to take a step out of bed without first examining the floor.

So the $1.75 Easter rabbit received a $20 hutch, and then extra wiring, and so on—the usual story of pet expenses. And became a part of our lives.

We tried various names, including the usual rabbit names like Thumper, but they didn't stick any more than all the contenders for re-naming Town Lake. So we called him Mr. Rabbit, since he seemed to demand rather than supplicate as most pets do.

Mr. Rabbit developed into a truly imperious individual. When he ran out of food and water, he would rattle his two crockery bowls until you had [to] put down the paper and go see to his needs. When you worked in the back yard, he would kick on the sides of his hutch till you turned him out. And if you were just passing through the yard and didn't speak, he would withdraw to the farthest corner of his hutch, turn his eyes away, and sulk till you left and returned. Even then, you had better speak softly, for he hated loud or sudden sounds and would refuse to come out of his hutch until the memory of the noisome intrusion had faded.

Only Mrs. Frantz could take him out of his hutch or put him back. Returning him was a neighborhood adventure in which he taunted us by dashing up under the porch, making us crawl to him on hands and knees, and then humiliating us by dashing right through our legs and stopping two feet behind to mock us. Despite what it did to middle-aged backs, we all enjoyed the contest.

Mr. Rabbit was pretty good about staying in the yard. Although our yard is fenced across the back, we have no fences between us and our neighbors on either side, just some pyracantha and oleander for borders. By and large those shrubs were his goal posts, and he seldom wandered out of the end zone. If I brought out a camera, he would become the impossible ham, particularly with that half-twist in mid-air to demonstrate his sheer joy of living. But if we ignored him, he woud de-weed the yard for awhile, and then find a place in the flower bed where he could smooth out a resting place and bed down till it was time to play the back-to-the-hutch game.

We have a Dalmatian named Pepe, an overgrown undertrained hulk of a hound. At first we feared for relations between the two, though we knew that, like Lenny in "Of Mice and Men," Pepe would injure something only through excessive affection. But Pepe's attitude became at once that of the proud, watchful uncle to Mr. Rabbit, sniffing a little now and then but never touching. Whenever we would miss Mr. Rabbit, and once we forgot and left him on the prowl for about nine hours, we would say, "Pepe, where's Mr. Rabbit?" And Pepe would spread his forelegs and point with his nose, which is all the pointing he has ever bothered to do.

And so this past week a writer-friend called that he had a manuscript ready for Eldon Branda and me to look at, and I made my once-a-year safari under the trees at Scholz, where we were all three unduly circumspect, so that I was home by 6:15 o'clock. As I was changing into leisure clothes, wondering whether to make one of my infrequent forays into yard work or walk Pepe through the waist-deep grass of Camp Mabry, I heard an unaccustomed high-pitched yapping with Pepe's hoarse bass as a dissonant obligato. Rushing outside, I saw two dogs—a red bird dog and a spotted grey one—rush from Mr. Rabbit's hutch and out of sight northward with all the speed they could muster.

Mr. Rabbit was in the corner of his hutch, breathing hard and huddled up. He looked at me with those round black eyes, but did not come forward to be petted. And then I saw the blood. And the fur. And one foot that had been dragged through his wire mesh floor and was lying on the ground.

Mrs. Frantz and a neighbor came at once with towels and a plastic tub, and we put Mr. Rabbit in it. The veterinarian, who did not know me, agreed to meet us at his clinic in fifteen minutes, and we hugged Mr. Rabbit close as we rushed to town. He responded to love as always, especially as he began to emerge from shock.

You know the end of the story. Three stumps chewed off at the elbow, and a monster slice across the belly. One half-paw left out of four. The veterinarian said he might be kept alive a little while but the foot-long tear, absolutely without hide, meant sure infection. There was no way.

So what? He was only a rabbit. A $1.75 one at that. Pets come, pets go.

Friends of mine have lost daughters in the past month, one in an accident, one in a murder. A Vietnamese photographer has just won a Pulitzer prize for his searing shot of that little girl running naked and crying down the road as she sheds her clothes, after a napalm raid by someone who never knew her.

Those people know real tragedy.

So, I can keep Mr. Rabbit in perspective. And I can turn down my neighbor's suggestion, blessed girl though she is, that she will sit on my back stoop all night with her shotgun in case those two at-large transients come smelling back to the scene of their crime. But the dogs, vicious though they were, aren't the miscreants. The crime goes back to the owners who let dogs loose in the world to prey on anything from flower beds to lesser animals to children and even adults. To owners who don't care.

No, my sadness lies in the uselessness of Mr. Rabbit's death. I see him, like that joke about the canaries in the back of the truck, trying to keep all four feet off his hutch floor while the demons nip and pull below, and I think of his terror as he realizes there is no escape.

Thus Mr. Rabbit joins the symbols. Of all the people in all the backyards of the world who are playing in their own hutches, peaceable and minding their own business, trying to find a more succulent reed or smoothing a spot from which to watch the world go by.

And along comes a wandering bully, or a whole pack of bullies. Not hungry but just looking for whatever excites at the moment. And utterly irresponsible. And no one seems to feel responsible. I was walking Pepe about a mile from home, along about 11 o'clock at night. It's a nice neighborhood, serene and buttoned-up and watered and manicured, though more poorly lighted than a Harlem slum. And a man had let his house dog out for the nightly run moment of truth, and Pepe and he had sniffed their amenities when out of the dark emerged a roving pack of five or six dogs and attacked Pepe. In trying to kick them off, I lost my balance and fell with the small of my back across the curb, cracking two vertebrae.

The resident, whom I know, came out, gathered his dog in, and went back inside. He never once looked to see whether I was some-one he knew, especially what I was doing lying on his curb at that time of night, nor how he could help. A bleeding dog and an aching owner walked an agonizing mile back to the house, where Mrs. Frantz and a neighbor scrubbed both of us before taking me on to Brackenridge's emergency ward. If we hadn't been playing Arkansas at Memorial Stadium that week-end, I probably would still be in bed. Instead, all I do is complain of my soft disc, which now and then warns me.

Are animals worth it? Should you have a pet if you have to keep it up? I would counter with the assertion that in this corporate mass of a world, we all need something to love that doesn't talk back, that responds, and that emphasizes only the most fundamental material needs. Pepe and I may argue over whether he is going to go down this trail or that one, but we never discuss Watergate or the City Council race or recruiting violations or the absence of reform in a world that cries for it. He wasn't even interested in the tree contro-versy that Frank Erwin kicked off several years ago, and if trees won't motivate him, nothing will.

But impersonality and neighbors who don't ask why you're lying on their curb are a minor part of the problem in a world that could be good.

The big problem that Mr. Rabbit symbolizes is the letting loose of terrors in the world without feeling concern for the consequences. This is not the place to try to be profound or complete, but merely to suggest. If Mr. Rabbit had died in Camp Mabry, if one of those too-fast cars that shoot all day and half the night down Edgemont and Balcones had run over him, if the April floods had brought pneumonia, Mr. Rabbit's death would have been our loss of a pet and no one else's concern.

But when he is where he is supposed to be, and the late spring sunshine is on the world, and the grass—his own plot—is green and juicy, should he, should any of us, have to feel embattled? Mr. Rabbit's castle was only a hutch, roofed over, with wire mesh on two sides for ventilation, and wire mesh for a floor, for obvious reasons. But it was his castle, and he was in it. And he was still invaded.

Like old women and children raped in their homes. Like Cambodian peasants who are looking for rice, not issues. Like Israeli athletes at Munich. Like Arabs in Jerusalem. Like everyone who is where he is supposed to be and is doing what he is supposed to be doing, and gets torn apart impersonally for no other reason than that he was eligible for invasion.

So much for the world at large. And back to mine. And to a fat round grey chuck of "chinchilla face . . . with a wiggle in your walk." I'm sorry you had to leave this way, Mr. Rabbit, though perhaps there's some cold comfort in knowing that for the last four miles of your 14 months of life, you were held close by someone who loves you.

Tribute to Richard T. Fleming at Memorial Services March 16, 1973

By Joe B. Frantz

On Monday morning I dropped by Dick Fleming's office to pick up this week's roster of enemies to be routed, bastions to be defended, and windmills to be tilted at. When his secretary, Maud Ann Armstrong, said he hadn't shown, we agreed that he had probably passed a book store en route and might not arrive till noon.

Shortly after, we learned that he had died earlier that morning sitting in his chair.

Checking back, we recreated his week-end—all day Friday at the annual meeting of the Texas State Historical Association visiting with friends of fifty years, all day Sunday playing with his adored, and adoring, grandchildren, talking with his son Jack, and then pottering about in the yard. Appropriately he had been active till the last. Dick Fleming was not born to let his last days ravel out. He left this world the way he must have entered it, and certainly the way he lived it—flank speed ahead, rudder hard over, all engines forward. No one was ever less intended for extended invalidism, for the pains and strains and diminutions of aging.

This article is reprinted from the *Library Chronicle* (of the University of Texas at Austin), New Series, VI (Dec., 1973), 16–23.

Dick did make a few concessions to time, but as few as possible, and each one grudgingly. The hands began to palsy a bit, the eyes watered more, the gold-headed cane which his grandfather brought from Ireland accompanied him everywhere. Lately he shuffled instead of spurted, but he still got there.

Once he *could* run. There was that melee in the latter days of the Johnson administration. Dick entered the Union, where an anti-military recruitment table had been set up.

"Is that a Viet Cong flag?" he asked one of the students.

Assured that it was, Dick grabbed the flag, split its pole over his knee, and stalked out with it. A huge student, whose one therapy class left him ample time to reform the world, gave chase. Out from the Union, up the mall, one round little body pursued by another a half-century younger and almost twice the height and breadth.

Youth won, the flag was grabbed away, and the victor started back to the Union. But Dick Fleming doesn't quit that easily. The chased—and with Dick the word would never be spelled c-h-a-s-t-e—ran after the chaser, caught him, and began to grapple again. The fight was uneven, but student bystanders intervened, captured the banner, and destroyed it.

A few minutes later, while Dick breathed like an accordion on a bench outside the Union, exuding a triumphantly apoplectic red halo, Dean Ed Price appeared on the run:

"I'm told there's a riot around here," he called.

"You're damned tooting there's a riot," Dick retorted between heaves. "And I'm it."

When somehow President Johnson heard of the incident, he wrote Dick that his was a courage that matched any soldier's in the field.

The students cherished him, even when they thought he was wrong. No further witness is needed than the space they gave him this past week in successive *Daily Texan*s. As Andy Yemma, a *Texan* editor of a couple of years ago, pointed out, he taught more students what life and the University were about than do most formal teachers.

It's difficult to talk about Dick Fleming without resorting to profanity, for he orchestrated strong language with all the sensitivity of a Toscanini or Bernstein, setting his audience up with a strong crescendo, and then, when it seemed their ears would burst, suddenly dropping off into a pianisimo of almost filigreed delicacy. On indignant notes the only time when he ever settled for less than High C came occasionally in mixed company when he'd reduce his oath to a pallid: "Oh, Garden Seed!" or, "for corn sake!" But even that concession carried no hint of fakery.

But Dick did abhor unnecessary obscenity, and he railed at the casual use of four-letter words by the New Generation. And a splendid feature of his blithe, happy turbulence was that he always acted or reacted as if he had invented the term "Direct Action."

On one memorable occasion Dick was returning from a favorite watering hole, the Forty Acres. Scrawled in paint on the sidewalk outside Hemphill's-on-the-Drag was the ultimate obscenity. How many disapproving nice persons must have tut-tutted the words as they walked by that day. But not Dick!

With one of the fastest-heating motors in the mobile world, he flashed into Hemphill's, waving his short arms and screaming for the manager. In a moment he was almost dragging a startled manager of Hemphill's out on the sidewalk, bucket of paint in one hand and brush in the other, and with Dick superintending, the offending words were painted into oblivion. Twenty minutes later some pedestrians must have been wondering why that big blotch of fresh red paint was defacing the busy sidewalk. As for Dick's friends, they were wondering how many more daily confrontations his system could take without blowing every gasket in his chunky body.

Dick also had no use for the gay liberation movement, though he confined his distaste to talk until on another day he saw the group handing out literature to some youth of high school age or younger.

If he had written what he said to the gay group on that occasion, the whole Drag would have had to be blotted with red.

Not all the memories are contemporary, but Dick could reminisce with vividness and fidelity mixed with intelligent sentimentality. He never reproduced static tableaux; rather, his memories resembled kinetic art, all animated and full of pulls and twists and squashings. And explosions.

Although none of us here was there, Dick could transport us to the time he was jailed in Nuevo Laredo because of a technicality involving his papers. For the Mexicans it must have been "The Ransom of Red Chief" re-enacted. "Oh, how I shook those bars and cussed," he would recall. "I used words I didn't know I knew."

Released, he tramped angrily across the international bridge into Laredo and hailed a taxi.

"Take me to Temple," he directed.

"Temple Avenue?" the driver asked.

"No, damn it! Temple, Texas!"

Six hundred and fifty miles later a tired, bewildered, but rewarded taxi driver re-entered Laredo, probably wondering whether his family would believe where he had been.

Or recall those gloomy political days in the 1920s when the Ku Klux Klan held power in Texas. One can see a young, dapper little man on the sidewalks of downtown Houston, inveighing so loudly against the hooded brethren that finally the city police hauled him off to jail. It was the only way they could figure to silence his protest against bigotry.

It's easy to resurrect in memory the Democratic National Convention in 1928 in Houston, bent on nominating Alfred E. Smith as the Democratic candidate. Equally determined were the evangelical Protestant denominations, holding round-the-clock prayer meetings to ward off this alleged disaster. And the secretary of the State Democratic Executive Committee, one Richard T. Fleming, marshalled all his eloquence and knowledge of both backroom and street maneuvering to nullify the churchmen. Although he lost that round, the opposition must have felt his sting.

Or that morbid, terrifying 1966 day of the Charles Whitman massacre from atop the University's Main Building. Just a few moments after Whitman started spraying bullets on the noon crowd, Dick's secretary received a call from her husband in the Tower. Since neither he nor anyone else was sure at that moment whether a single gunman or a whole platoon had taken over, her husband cautioned her not to leave the Academic Center. She warned Dick.

With his instinctive high gear he ran out of the office and up the stairs to wave away the departing students and staff from the exits. Then he thought of the second floor reading room with all of its glass. He almost leaped up the stairs and burst into the room, yelling at the top of his voice for everyone to get away from the windows: "They're killing people out there!"

From behind a desk a pleasant little librarian came rushing at him, fingers to her lips, shusing him.

"Damn it, woman," he cried out, "there's a madman loose in the Tower."

Then he started shouting again: "Get back! Get down! You'll be shot, damn you all!"

By this time she had caught up to him, and in a desperate whisper, finger still to her lips, admonished:

"You'll have to leave. You can't talk like that in here. This is a LIBRARY!"

Later, under less serious circumstances, Dick liked to tell this story, finger exaggeratedly at his lips, terminating invariably with a bit of philosophizing—"It's reassuring as all hell to know that some people maintain standards. We could have had bodies and blood all over the floor, but by damn, she'd keep her library quiet!"

Or that great week in Manhattan when he was supping at another favorite bistro, Le Cheval Blanc. Glancing up from his companions, he noticed that the place lacked any painting of a white horse, Gauguin's masterpiece or otherwise. According to his account, and I checked it out two decades later with the proprietor and the bartender, he pounded the bar and demanded as only Dick Fleming could demand when his outrage was triggered. The bartender, taken aback, charged:

"If you're so hot for a white horse, why don't you paint it yourself?"

"I will; by gad, I will indeed," Dick shouted—and left forthwith. For nights on end he painted furiously. From this freshet of creativity emerged the Richard T. Fleming delineation of *Le Cheval Blanc*, derivative perhaps, but good enough that a quarter century later it still hangs there, dead center above and behind the bar, with a bold and unmistakable Fleming signature.

"I'm really Grandpa Moses," he used to say with an admixture of pride and deprecation. "But if Churchill and Eisenhower can get away with it, why can't I?"

Then there is the picture of Richard and Harriet Fleming, denizens of the silk stocking, rock-ribbed Republican community of Rye, New York, deciding that the time had come for the local Democratic party, in more disarray than usual, to assert itself. They learned what political types had failed to notice—Rye has strong ethnic minorities, particularly Italians. And so Dick and Harriet stuffed themselves at spaghetti-and-Chianti suppers night after stupefying night until on election day the city chose the first Democratic mayor in memory, perhaps in history. According to Dick, "After that, it was some years before we could tolerate spaghetti again, and Rye reverted to the Grand Old Party." The way he flattened his lips on those last three words was hardly complimentary.

There is that autumn in 1931 when Dick arranged a special train and cudgeled all possible Texas alumni in the New York sector to carry the torch of Southwestern football honor to the gates of Harvard Stadium. But, alas, the Longhorns, weary from almost three days on the train, lost by four touchdowns, and in Dick's words, "I was so humiliated that for days I felt that every shoeshine boy and every waitress in mid-town Manhattan was looking down on me." Actually I don't believe that, for it is my observation that Dick's effervescence would bubble through in a matter of moments. Lasting humiliation did not harmonize with his belligerent zest.

Dick Fleming was a character—individual and sometimes outrageous and irrepressible and often unmanageable. But in a world in which we seem increasingly stamped out like interchangeable parts, he was unique. His interests were wide-ranging, as one glance at his cluttered office and library, which spills over into every room in his three-story house, will demonstrate. Although he loved to travel, he refused to learn to drive, which meant that his wife logged more hours on European and Mexican highways than an airline pilot. He loved sports and art and music and ballet. But mostly he loved to read and talk and persuade.

The combination of knowledge, articulateness, and persuasiveness carried him a long way. From the son of a railroad engineer in Temple; through a distinguished student career at The University of Texas and a love affair with that institution that endured to the end; to the First Officers Training Corps at Leon Springs and eventual rank as a major; to becoming one of the organizers of the Houston Oil Company, a major independent for forty years; and on to vice-president and general counsel of Texas Gulf Sulphur.

"Dick, how did you ever survive as the lone Democrat on Texas Gulf's board of directors?"

"Oh, he'd reply, "those characters—and "characters" is a euphemism—"Those characters never knew what I was talking about! Besides, they panicked when the New Deal came on, and I was the only one who kept my head!"

When on one December night in Washington, D.C., in 1958, Walter Prescott Webb gave the presidential address to the American Historical Association, Dick Fleming came down on the train to hear it, the first time I met him. Parenthetically, I was struck that any corporation vice-president would travel to Washington to hear a historian—I would have been impressed if he had traveled crosstown in Austin!

It turned out to be like many a late lunch and evening together over the next fifteen years. At midnight Walter Webb dropped out, almost with Dick's blessing, since Webb had asked for a glass of milk in a Washington bar. At 3 o'clock in the morning I begged off, with Dick shouting about the softness of the younger generation and demanding to know whatever had happened to the sturdy spirit of the American pioneer.

But he forgave my defection, and we grew closer together through visits in Austin and New York. And then one day he queried me from New York: would the University be interested in 250 packing boxes of books and pamphlets by University ex-students that he had been collecting over the years? Harry Ransom settled that question before I could finish asking him, and shortly Dick Fleming was installed as a nothing-a-year man in the Main Building and then later in the Academic Center.

Over the next dozen years he begged, threatened, cajoled, and otherwise conned ex-students and faculty out of their creations—and as a group they don't give easily. If his pay had been at his accustomed level, the cost would have been astronomical. Even at librarian's scale he contributed possibly a couple of hundred thousand dollars' worth of time. Once I asked him how much of the collection he had bought personally:

"Joe," he said, "I realize I'm passing up a tax break, but I've never kept records. I didn't want to know how much I was spending for these books, because I was afraid it might inhibit me." But one thing

I can assert—his personal expenditures ran into the tens of thousands.

He was always a little hurt, though not surprised, that he was never named a Distinguished Alumnus. Mainly the award goes to distinguished Establishment types. By accomplishment Richard Fleming belonged to the Establishment, but by nature he was a rebel.

But he knew that many appreciated him, as witness this excerpt from a 1970 note which Harry Ransom wrote:

"I stand in admiration, of course, when I think of your career; but in deeper, more personal, more lasting ways I stand in gratitude for your gift of your life to this University. I wish I could tell you how much sense and determination and clarity your being 'with us' has brought to these last years. . . ."

Thus he rode the Austin city buses, arguing and agreeing with the maids and the yardmen; he fought furiously with the administration and many alumni over burnt orange versus regular orange, a battle that he lost, though like Goldwater in 1964, he never conceded; he fired off letters and shouted over the telephone at every sinner; and he attended Regents' meetings, where he exercised his right of free speech. Just last week in Dallas, Rabbi Levi Olan, a former Regent, talked about Dick to me: "He was a nuisance, but you know, we sometimes needed a nuisance."

Dick loved a worthy antagonist, and he found one in Frank Erwin, with whom he tangled at every opportunity. Actually the two scrappers were very alike; an observation which both would deny vehemently and profanely. And nothing pleased Dick more than when after one particularly acerbic interchange, Erwin sent him a hand-written apology. He must have shown it to me at least once every two months, along with his fat walletful of speakeasy cards that he had carried daily since 1933, "just in case."

Three more short, final glimpses of this remarkable spirit, this rampaging fighter against cant and hypocrisy and covert actions, this creature of extreme dignity and sometimes Victorian courtesy and genteelness, this bundle of emotion and pride and drive.

One portrait takes place at the Forty Acres Club, where he threw his own 80th birthday party three years ago this coming April 12. Although he invited old friends to lunch at noon, we didn't begin to eat till almost mid-afternoon. He was eloquent, and he was not the least ashamed to tell each and every one how dearly he loved us. On his next two birthdays he and I ate alone, because as he said, "I can't go through that sort of emotional wringing for another eighty years!"

Another occurred this past December when the Philosophical Society of Texas met at the Hilton Inn in Dallas. Like all meetings, it was a bit of an endurance contest, and most people were ready to turn in after the dinner speech. As Mrs. Frantz and I walked through the lobby en route to the elevator, there sat Dick looking bellicose.

"Something wrong, Dick?"

"Spurned!" he said. (He made the word sound somehow obscene.) "Spurned! I'm never coming to another of these—everyone but me has gotten too everlasting old to enjoy himself!"

So we went with Dick to the hotel lounge, picking up Ed and Anne Clark on the way, thereby enhancing the prospect of good, competitive talk. About midnight the Clarks and the Frantzs were frankly tired, and excused themselves. But by then Dick had gathered a fresh group of auditors and hardly seemed to notice our going.

Through all this hyperactivity Dick had a wife and son who understood him—his faults, which he almost paraded; and his strengths, about which he was frequently diffident. Later, from his own remarks, I gather that both his daughter-in-law and grandchildren recognized that he was more than a little special.

When he and Harriet married, Dick said they agreed that they would never tell the same story twice about either their backgrounds or about how they met. From the Fleming folklore that I have gathered from their casual acquaintances, they undoubtedly kept their vows.

They married after a post–World War I romance that saw her in Alaska and him in the District of Columbia, and evidently they had only one or two dates over a three-year period. But they agreed to meet and marry in New Orleans. Typically, on the train over from Houston Dick met a couple of men, strangers both, told them where he was heading, and they took charge of the wedding arrangements on arrival. During the service at the Hotel Roosevelt a tiny tad of a lad stole into the ceremony, took Dick by the hand, and stood between the bride and groom throughout the entire rites, with Dick squeezing the boy's hand tightly.

He held a lot of our hands over the years, and less often we held his. He had his heroes—like Edmund Heinsohn, H. J. Ettlinger, Robert L. Moore, J. R. Parten, Charles Sparenbergy, Leonard Kreisle, Frances Hudspeth, Leon Green, Donald Weisman, and most especially, Harry Ransom. And he had others who have preceded him, like Walter Webb, Stanley Walker, Edmunds Travis, Will Hogg, Frank Dobie, John W. Thomason, John A. Lomax, and Harry Benge Crozier. All were men who have or had ranged widely, but never attained the weariness of cynicism nor enjoyed the luxury of negativism.

Looking back, it's not Dick Fleming's fault that he didn't save the world from its folly. He spent eighty-three indignant years trying, and never once did he falter in his faith nor surrender his dream.

Just last week he and Mrs. Fleming had their wedding anniversary, and though the facts were against it, Dick talked to her about how as soon as she was able, they would take one more long trip and just enjoy each other. Although such talk may not be realistic, it expresses the truth of his life.

So now the loud voice has grown quiet and the restless, questing, questioning spirit serene. And no longer can a boring day be sal-

vaged by fueling Dick's indignation. And no more will the belligerent, jaunty figure in the Harris tweed and old-fashioned railroaders'
watch and Sherlock Holmes hat wait outside the Co-op for the
evening bus.

For the feasts and frolics of old days together will have vanished.
And these good times and these good battles and these defeats and
these occasional victories will never come back again. But Richard T.
Fleming burned his spirit deep into our souls, and when tomorrow
we ride out again on a new morning's wind, we'll carry him with
us right to our own journey's end. And the world will be less grey
because of the greenness of his once-presence and now the salt and
savor of his memory.

Opening a Curtain: The Metamorphosis of Lyndon B. Johnson

BY JOE B. FRANTZ*

Two decades ago a young lawyer friend of mine wound up in Houston with one of those huge law corporations with multiple partners, all with acceptable Anglo-Saxon names except the one at the tag end of the letterhead. The firm's name was something like Fulbright, Crooker, Bates, Freeman, and Jaworski. As my friend observed to me, "Obviously, Jaworski made it on merit." (This was before Leon Jaworski became Public Enemy No. 1 on the Richard Milhous Nixon Enemies List.)

I bring this story up only because I have been looking over the list of past presidents of the Southern Historical Association, and I can only surmise that most of them made it on merit. I don't make that claim for myself.

While I cannot identify the brand that the nominations committee was imbibing the night it chose me, I do accept its shaky judgment and say merely, "Here I am, undoubtedly the least southern of your presidents in the otherwise long and honorable history of this

---

This article is reprinted from *The Journal of Southern History,* 45 (Feb., 1979).

*Mr. Frantz is professor of history at the University of Texas at Austin. This paper was delivered as the presidential address at the annual meeting of the Southern Historical Association in St. Louis, Missouri, on November 9, 1978.

Association." My only claim to merit is genuine service on most of the SHA committees, especially the one once named to find a successor to Bennett H. Wall. After an exhaustive search we reported that there is no successor to—or substitute for—our reed of an executive secretary. That recommendation represents one of my rare right decisions, as well as a refusal to fly in the face of facts.

But I do have some credentials for what I am going to discuss with you tonight. For six years I pursued the trail of former President Lyndon Baines Johnson, tape recorder ready, seeing friend and foe alike, until my staff and I had some 1,200 interviews in hand. To date, no other President has been captured from as many aspects as was President Johnson by his contemporaries. What matters is that we examined hundreds of witnesses who revealed facets of a man who served in Washington under one-sixth of all the Presidents, including himself, whose service was frequently significant and high level, and whose impact on the nation, whether for good or ill, will last most or all of our lives.

Oral history, as you know, is one of the newer adjuncts of the historical profession, with obvious advantages. Oral history holds the advantage of effortlessness. Most people talk more easily than they write. They talk more freely, more naturally. They freeze when they become self-conscious. Even scholars, who presumably write as part of their profession, suffer from this malady, as witness the turgid prose issuing from so many semisomnolent typewriters.

Consequently, we have in the Lyndon B. Johnson Presidential Library ten million or more words that would likely have never found their way into the record, words that represent a sort of stream-of-consciousness approach to history as seen by eyewitnesses, words and thoughts that were articulated in usually relaxed situations, words that illumine the frequently opaque hard facts with which our profession deals.

As I have pondered these millions of words, several insights have emerged. For our purposes here one idea that stands apart and that deserves examination is the generally consistent development of Lyndon B. Johnson from a young politician who mirrored the strengths and biases of his central Texas homeland to a mature politician who upended for the nation the greatest cornucopia of social legislation in its history.

Where did Johnson's social concern stem from? Why did he become so nationally concerned that his base of strength, the South, turned against him, to the point of refusing to place the Democratic party—its historic friend, Johnson's party—on the ballot in several states in the presidential election of 1968? Why, as in 1964, had he already taken such alleged antisouthern actions in his brief Presidency that in that campaign year he readily conceded that Barry Morris Goldwater's greatest strength lay in the South? Why was his wife's whistle-stop campaign through her native South met with such occasional hostility?

Before we start chasing answers to these questions in earnest, let us diverge for one more suggestion. The South is currently booming, generally the most rapidly advancing section of the nation under its booster title of the Sun Belt. Vitality seems to ooze from its black soil and its red clay and from its pine forests and even its sluggish streams. The stereotype of the lazy southerner has disappeared from contemporary folklore, except as it may linger in the emotions of a few outside observers who have been Rip Van Winkling for the past twenty years or so. And in 1976, when we witnessed the election of a man from the Deep South, from a country town called Plains, no less, most pundits agreed that his election was made possible by overwhelming majorities from southern blacks. Yet only a dozen years before Johnson himself had confided to Walter Wilson Jenkins, as the President debated whether to run for a full term or retire, "I just don't think a white Southerner is a man to unite this nation. . . ."[1]

---

[1] Johnson, *The Vantage Point: Perspectives of the Presidency, 1963–1969* (New York, 1971), 97.

Nor was Johnson the only person who felt so strongly about his being shut out from the Presidency because of his birth in the old Confederacy. Robert Jackson, a Texan from Corpus Christi then in Washington, tells how thirty years earlier he and his wife invited a newly arrived Johnson to their apartment. Johnson kept the pair awake most of the night talking, which led Mrs. Jackson to remark to her weary husband that their guest would probably be President some day. "I told her how stupid she was," recalled Jackson, "and how little she knew about politics, because nobody from Texas would ever be President."[2]

But in the past two decades we have come a long way in uniting the South with the remainder of the nation. Similarly, we have advanced in convincing the remainder of the nation and the world that the South is made up of human beings instead of ghostly left-overs in crinoline and string ties who eat blacks for breakfast and genuflect every time the name of Robert Edward Lee is mentioned. And no one did more to engineer this change in attitudes than Lyndon B. Johnson, who by the very nature of his background should have been designated as the least likely person to pull off such a revolution.

To be a southerner in politics was to invite a similar discrimination as practiced nationally against blacks and women. None of the three groups could aspire to the Presidency.

As far back as 1953, when Johnson was a fairly new minority leader of the United States Senate, he told a *Time* magazine reporter that he did not aspire to the Presidency, because, as he said, "I come from the wrong part of the country."[3] And in 1960 he persuaded Sam Rayburn and John Bowden Connally to shut down the presi-

[2] Interview, David G. McComb with Robert Jackson, Corpus Christi, Texas, Oral History Project, University of Texas at Austin. Tape and transcript are in the Lyndon Baines Johnson Presidential Library, Austin, Texas. The interviews took place between September 1968 and August 1974. All interviews cited hereinafter are in the same depository and are from the Oral History Project. The library will hereinafter be cited as LBJL.

[3] *Time*, LXI (June 22, 1953), 23.

dential campaign headquarters they had opened in Washington without his permission on the plea that "a Southerner could not, and probably should not, be elected."[4]

But Johnson did become President, as we know. Although it took a murder in Dallas, he made it to the White House. And afterwards he was elected to a full term, paving the way for James Earl "Jimmy" Carter. And meanwhile the nation witnessed the 1964 phenomenon of Johnson *versus* Goldwater, neither candidate from a state that traditionally supplies candidates and both from almost contiguous states that are tucked away in the southwestern corner of the United States. And eight years later South Dakota, with an even smaller population base, gave us one of the major presidential candidates in George Stanley McGovern. Perhaps we have begun to become the "land of the free," where any mother's son or daughter can dream of becoming President with some hope of achieving that goal. And once we cross each color and sex line, the second attempt will follow as easily as nominating Catholic John Fitzgerald Kennedy after Catholic Alfred Emanuel Smith, or sending Henry B. Gonzalez back to Congress from San Antonio for term after term or Edward William Brooke to the Senate from Massachusetts or Barbara C. Jordan from Houston for as long as she chose to remain—or electing as President the Georgian after the Texan. Maybe we will become a land of people finally.

But that is not my focus here tonight. Let's look more specifically at Johnson.

As the 1960s approached nationally syndicated cartoonists had their usual field day with unannounced presidential candidate Lyndon B. Johnson, the majority leader of the United States Senate. They depicted him, stretching his long frame over at least nine feet of height, looking still taller in a high-crowned, wide-brimmed

---

[4] Johnson, *The Vantage Point*, 90.

Stetson and high-heeled, hand-tooled cowboy boots. He was [a] typical Texan, whatever that image conveys, and the words that issued
from his ample mouth were pure Texanese, as western as John
Wayne, except that each sentence invariably ended with the phrase
"you all," a concession to his southernism. Sometimes one boot
would be planted firmly in West Texas, the other in the spongy soil
of the Deep South. All that was lacking were the Sons of the Pio-
neers singing "Cool Water" in one corner and blacks strumming
mandolins as darkness gathered on the delta—any delta—in the
opposite corner.

The cartoons showed Johnson's dilemma. Was he a western candidate or was he a southern one? Or was he, as most cartoonists hint-
ed, trying to straddle both sections, utilizing his Texas background
to illustrate his transitional position? Never mind. You could accept
him as belonging to one section or the other, or to both; but you
never suggested that he represented the nation.

Other cartoons showed Adlai Ewing Stevenson wrestling in his
eloquent way with Middle East and Russian problems; William
Stuart Symington represented military problems; John F. Kennedy,
labor and management; Hubert Horatio Humphrey, the minorities
and the dispossessed. Each had national concerns involving national
constituencies. But Johnson represented only the South and the
West, when he wasn't representing the petroleum industry. To politicians and voters he remained a regional candidate, despite his national position as Senate majority leader. And when he was placed on the
ticket as vice-presidential running mate with John F. Kennedy, the
press quite correctly still looked on his selection as a device to hold
the South in the party. Meanwhile, loyal Democrats like Walter Philip
Reuther, G. Mennen Williams, and Robert Francis Kennedy protest-
ed his selection because of his presumed narrowness.[5] He was a

---

[5] Ibid., 92.

regional man, nothing he could do would release him from that straitjacket.

Actually, this attitude toward Johnson was erroneous, though it had emotional authenticity because of his style and the nation's attitude toward Texas and the South. Without attempting to equate Johnson with more distinguished antecedents, public reaction to the man and to many more of similar background reminds one of the Biblical question: "Can . . . any good thing come out of Nazareth?" Could any good come out of Texas?

But from the first Johnson had shown certain progressive and even liberal tendencies, so that his performance as President remains consistent with his actions of the past. His Great Society does not represent a break with his past and is not, as charged by many contemporary southern leaders, an aberration, an alleged sellout to the votes of blacks and northern liberals.

Take, for instance, Johnson's very first noticeability in Washington. The year is 1933, the first spring of the New Deal, and Johnson is a twenty-four-year-old secretary to a Texas congressman, Richard Mifflin Kleberg, Sr. In that year Johnson led an "open revolt against the conduct of 'the Little Congress' (the secretarial organization modeled after Congress) by an 'oligarchy' of veteran members." A majority of the other secretaries named Johnson as their new speaker. Throughout the five-paragraph story in the Washington *Star* the victory for Johnson was trumpeted as a triumph of liberals over "standpatters" in "the most lively" sessions held by the Little Congress to that time. And the new speaker, borrowing from the nation's new symbol, promised all the secretaries a "new deal for all Little Congresses."[6]

Even before then, as a college youngster dropping out to recoup his finances teaching at Cotulla, Texas, Johnson had adumbrated his

---

[6] Washington *Evening Star*, April 28, 1933.

future Head Start program, more than forty years down the road. With a student body that was heavily Mexican-American and correspondingly deprived, he had written his mother to send him two hundred packages of toothpaste for his student body of 250.[7] And as Congressman Kleberg's secretary Johnson evidently prevailed on his employer to support the World War I veterans' bonus, the proposed Agricultural Adjustment Administration, and the projected regulation of holding companies, bills toward which Kleberg apparently had little affirmative inclination.[8]

Robert Clifton Weaver, the first secretary of housing and urban development as well as the first black cabinet member ever, once told the present speaker that he first heard of Lyndon B. Johnson when Weaver, Ralph Johnson Bunche, and other young black intellectuals in Washington began to get word that down in Texas a state National Youth Administration director in his mid-twenties was spending money and dreaming up projects that benefited, in Weaver's words, "Negroes and poor white folks." Such a practice was unheard of in most states, where the NYA chiefly helped young people whose social and political clout was well known. Weaver said that though the name Lyndon Johnson meant nothing to him then, he decided that he should keep an eye on this unique person from this strange faraway land.

From Houston came a report from Beatrice Denmark, saying that in Texas she had "found what I have been hoping to find for colored girls. . . . The Texas Director is doing what many of us are talking."[9] Three months later, just after Johnson was elected to his first congressional term, that angel of the modern black movement, Mary McLeod Bethune, wrote Johnson

---

[7] Johnson to Mrs. Sam E. Johnson, October 17, 1928, LBJL.

[8] Interview, McComb with Jackson, Corpus Christi, Texas.

[9] Denmark to Richard R. Brown, February 9, 1937, United States Government Records, NYA 1935–1938, Box 6, Administrative Reports, June–September 1936, LBJL.

that the same energy and vigorous imagination that characterized the out-standing success of your program with the National Youth Administration will write your name high in the annals of the House of Rep[resentatives].

We are indeed happy that one who has proven himself so conscious of and sympathetic with the needs of all the people should take his place in a Congress that is so indelibly writing a more human and more Christian con-cept of American democracy.[10]

When Johnson announced for Congress in 1937 Aubrey Willis Williams, national director of the NYA, called on President Franklin Delano Roosevelt to dissuade the young Texan, saying that Johnson was more important as state NYA director than he could ever be as a Texas congressman. (He probably thought, as I sometimes do in consonance with the remainder of the nation, that there are too many Texas congressmen already.) But Roosevelt demurred because Johnson was running on a platform promising all-out support to the President, even though the Texas delegation, ranging from the Texas vice president John Nance Garner down to local Texas offi-cials, were all making political hay out of damning the New Deal. Roosevelt was not going to discourage a potential congressman from Texas who evidently would follow him all the way to the well.[11]

When four years later Johnson made his first run at elective office, again he joined the liberal wing of his party. Whether his liberality stemmed from conviction or merely represented shrewd politics can be debated, but no question exists as to the astuteness and direction of his move. Running against a double handful of opponents for the unexpired congressional term of James Paul Buchanan of the Tenth District of Texas, Johnson endorsed the New Deal down the line, including the reorganization package of the United States Supreme Court, which had set Texans' political teeth on edge. Some of the

---

[10] Bethune to Johnson, May 3, 1937, House of Representatives Papers, Box 2, "B", LBJL.

[11] Interview, Joe B. Frantz with Thomas G. Corcoran, Washington, D.C.

other candidates opposed the "packing bill," as its foes dubbed it. Johnson reasoned correctly that his opponents would split the anti–New Deal vote among themselves, while he should receive most of the pro-Franklin D. Roosevelt votes. Since he needed only a plurality, if he could segregate the Rooseveltians into his camp, he should win. That is the way the script read, and that is the way he produced it. Although campaign money lay heavily with those disenchanted Texans who were beginning to view Roosevelt as some sort of anti-Christ, the beleaguered New Dealers in Texas stayed with Johnson and put him officially and electively in Washington for the next nearly 12,000 days.

Of course, when the Supreme Court reorganization went down to defeat, in large part because of the opposing leadership of the Texas congressional delegation, the spotlight shone on the twenty-eight-year-old maverick who had refused to run with the Texas herd. His stance guaranteed at least minimum name recognition in the nation's press for the new congressman, and it brought him to the attention of no less a person than Roosevelt himself, who was in a position to appreciate and reward party loyalty.

And Johnson soon proved to be more than a one-issue New Dealer. In that first session he helped forward to completion such progressive measures as the Lower Colorado River Authority ("Texas' little TVA," in the words of Benjamin Victor Cohen), the Pedernales rural-electrification cooperative, the Brazos River flood-control plan, a bill to reduce farm tenancy (all measures aimed at increasing farm income and farm relief), and crop-control legislation. And wonder of wonders—for a Texas representative—he supported the wages and hours bill, which he defended as helping to eliminate abuses existing in industry. To the charge that the bill would discourage industries from moving to the South, Johnson answered: "If an industry cannot pay decent wages, I do not want it in my district." At this statement the Austin Chamber of Commerce fathers must have aged perceptibly.

Meanwhile Johnson's concern for the plight of the black spilled over into his first term as congressman. As a freshman congressman he obtained an appointment with President Roosevelt himself, his purpose being to complain about Milo Randolph Perkins, head of the Agricultural Adjustment Administration, the old Triple A. Although Perkins was one of the administration's stalwarts, Johnson told Roosevelt that Perkins was not passing on AAA benefits to Negro farmers in Texas. According to Grace Tully, Roosevelt's "first automatic instinct was, 'Now this is a smart politician.' And then he realized . . . that this was the day of the lily-white primary in Texas; and that contrary to the idea of adding votes or adding to the political career of Congressman Johnson, this might even backfire on him."[12]

That record, those concerns could have represented the forthrightness of a young, new congressman who hadn't yet fallen under the spell of Sam Rayburn's famous dictum: "To get along, you've got to go along." After all, Johnson was just finishing out a dead man's term. The test would come when he ran for a full term. Then the voters could see who would vote conviction and who would vote constituency.

That test came rather quickly. Senate Bill 2475 came over to the House of Representatives in 1938 and was quickly bottled up in the Committee on Rules. The bill placed a floor of twenty-five cents an hour on the wages of certain workers. The outcry in opposition to the bill was almost deafening. To its enemies it represented a definite concession to socialism, if not communism. To them it meant the ruination of the United States as it was then understood. It guaranteed the end of free, private enterprise in this nation, the termination of the southern way of life, and the destruction of Christianity and motherhood. When in May 1938 House Resolution 478 was voted

---

[12] Interview, Thomas Harrison Baker with Ernest Goldstein, Washington, D.C.

on to discharge the Committee on Rules from considering HR 478 by making the Senate bill a special order of business, Johnson joined the five others as the only six Texas congressmen with the courage to back the bill. In Texas they were told that their stances assured their defeat in the upcoming congressional elections.

Their critics proved one-third correct. When the next congressional elections were held Fontaine Maury Maverick and William Doddridge McFarlane were no longer members of Congress. But Johnson survived, and as he admitted years later, "I don't know what happened to me except I didn't have an opponent."[13] Johnson, who often told this story, conveniently forgot three of the Texans who voted with him—Sam Rayburn, Albert Thomas, and Robert Ewing Thomason. The story sounds better if he is the only one surviving, and Johnson had the instincts of a good storyteller who doesn't permit details to damage his impact. Although eastern politicians, labor leaders, and much of the national press praised the Texas sextet, the risk politically was hardly worth the accolades.

With Roosevelt running for an unprecedented third term in 1940 the Democratic leadership feared that a backlash might develop against senators and representatives seeking reelection by those Democrats who opposed breaking the two-term tradition for Presidents. At one time the White House feared losing as many as twelve seats in Illinois, five in Indiana, and three in Missouri. The Middle West promised to develop into a congressional disaster area. When, on the advice of Sam Rayburn and James H. Rowe, Roosevelt designated Johnson, still chronologically young at thirty-two years, to head the committee to rescue the threatened Democratic congressmen, no one questioned whether he came from the South or from Texas but whether he could get the job done. As Robert Sharon Allen was to write at the end of the campaign, "Lyndon performed miracles,"

[13] Joe B. Frantz, *37 Years of Public Service: The Honorable Lyndon B. Johnson* (Austin, 1974), n.p.

meanwhile complimenting the congressman for his "enlightened view."[14]

Again, at the conclusion of World War II Johnson warned Texas legislators in a special ceremony at the state capitol in Austin that the soldiers who have "tasted achievement will never again be content with the mild tea of generous promises." He added, "In a democracy the greatest cannot rise far above the most humble. Were those men alive today who formed Texas they would say to us '. . . Lead our people up . . . and up. Bring to them education. . . . sound minds in sound bodies. For the progress of men is limited only by the backwardness of men'."[15]

This was strong talk to a home constituency which still believed that the American way of life was superior to any other in the world because it provided its citizens with more bathtubs, more telephones, and more automobiles. Many legislators groused that Johnson had confused democracy with equality, a dangerous misconception in a state that dotes on its status quo.

By the next year Johnson was sounding even more dangerous. Along with lonely President Harry S Truman, Johnson was espousing federal assistance to health care—"socialized medicine," as its fearful opponents labeled the proposal. Charged Johnson: ". . . all of the talk about socializing medicine is nonsense and should be laid on the table. . . ." What the nation needed, added Johnson, was more doctors and nurses—Texas, he pointed out, was 1,400 doctors short for its population. The people were exercised over the wrong concerns—they worried about the doctors, not the patients, he declared. Talking in those plain terms that his critics would later decry, but terms nonetheless that people can understand, Johnson turned specific in his advocacy: ". . . the fly which eats at the open privy of a slum area has no scruples about carrying polio to the child in the

---

[14] Allen to Sam Rayburn, November 7, 1940 (copy), LBJL.

[15] Untitled speech, Austin, December 28, 1945, typescript, LBJL.

silk-stocking area. . . . The health of a community can be no better than the health of those least able to afford medical and hospital care."[16]

But the idea of federal assistance to proper health care was too far ahead of its time and would wait another two decades—until Johnson himself was President—before it would become a merciful fact. But again Johnson was being consistent.

Up to now in this narrative Johnson has looked good, a somewhat radical agrarian from a land of worn-out soil and poor crops in sequence who had transferred some of that radicalism to larger problems. But Johnson's good record has its flip side, and this other side does him scant credit.

The year was 1946, the boys had returned from the war, and American manufacturing and selling of consumer goods had resumed its upward trend. Organized labor, only a decade old in political acceptance, was resolved to obtain its share of the prospective wealth, while management was equally resolute in pursuing its desires. The nation was turning conservative, a turn that Texas did not need to make since it had disliked New Deal social and labor gains since good times, never very far away, had begun to return early in the Roosevelt era. The prevailing mood in Texas and the South was decidedly antilabor, though organized labor in Texas was not without its clout.

The big issue in 1946 was the Taft-Hartley Act, passed by a Congress determined to redress the alleged imbalance between labor and management. Labor denounced the act as slave-labor legislation, a bit of overreaction but not without a certain justification. Johnson voted for the Taft-Hartley Act, Truman vetoed it, and Congress promptly overrode the veto. Johnson again voted against his party's leadership and against labor.

---

[16] "Not That Men Shall Die, but That Men May Live," *Congressional Record*, 79 Cong., 2 Sess., Appendix, A2153–55 (April 13, 1946).

Organized labor, hitherto somewhat in his camp, as promptly denounced Johnson, and labor's opposition very nearly cost him his
first election as United States senator two years later in that famous
eighty-seven-vote campaign. Why did Johnson take such a chance
with annoying one of his chief supports? For one thing, the district
he represented as well as the people he most nearly claimed as his
political friends in Congress, were all against the steadily rising influence of labor since the Wagner Act—"Labor's Magna Carta"—had
been passed in 1935. Good central Texas politics demanded a vote
for Taft-Hartley. But organized labor had invariably supported him,
and for him to turn his back on labor in this crucial instance is difficult to justify.

William S. White, an appreciative biographer of Johnson, says that
the Taft-Hartley does not represent a backward step for Johnson in
his public thinking, but simply "a change in the realities which under-
lay . . . [the times]."[17]

The President's brother, less blindly devoted in his admiration,
does not entirely concur. According to Sam Houston Johnson, then
assisting his congressman brother, he had prepared a press release
attacking the Taft-Hartley bill, when Congressman Johnson told his
younger brother to scrub it. Sam Houston Johnson writes that he
could hardly believe his ears. "You can't do that," he told his brother. "Damn it, Lyndon, that's an antilabor law. The unions will crucify
you!"

"Have you read the bill, Sam Houston?" LBJ asked, adding that if
he had not, which indeed Sam Houston had not, he had "better read
it before . . . [going] off halfcocked. . . . it isn't what labor says it is.
It's a good law, and I'm voting for it."

Sam Houston remonstrated with his erring brother, telling him
that his vote would cost him 300,000 labor votes and probably the

---

[17] White, *The Professional: Lyndon B. Johnson* (Boston and Cambridge, 1964), 155.

upcoming senatorial race. Johnson replied that "The working people know better than that." In that case, the younger brother was wiser politically, and most historians woud agree that he was also more judicious socially. But organized labor in Texas turned on Johnson, and in Sam Houston's terms, "went all-out against him" because of his Taft-Hartley vote.[18] The result was that in the primary Johnson ran more than 71,000 votes behind his principal opponent, Coke Robert Stevenson, and in the runoff he just barely sneaked in with the notorious eighty-seven-vote margin. The irony is that Stevenson had no concern whatsoever for labor, a fact that was well known, but as governor of Texas at the time that Taft-Hartley became an issue he did not have to declare himself on the measure. Johnson, in short, was punished for taking a stance which he probably could not avoid.

On the other hand, Allan Shivers, former governor of Texas, thinks that Johnson's more conservative approach to the election of 1948, including his vote for Taft-Hartley, brought him enough conservative votes to enable him to squeeze home by the narrow margin. "I think that one thing alone enabled Johnson to get close enough in votes to where the Jim Wells box could make the difference," says Shivers.[19]

As we Tex-Mex types shrug, "*Quien sabe?*" Who knows?

Later, as Senate minority leader Johnson atoned slightly for his earlier support of the Taft-Hartley. When the Republicans under Dwight David Eisenhower decided to strengthen the act in the 1950s Johnson had every one of the Democrats sitting in his seat— "just an unheard-of thing," according to Kenneth Milton Birkhead, who adds that "when the vote started . . . he had every one of them, including Harry Byrd of Virginia, and some real mavericks in the party ready to vote to hold back on these amendments. I think it was one of the most dramatic highlights of his career as leader of the

---

[18] Johnson, *My Brother Lyndon* (New York, 1970), 74–75.
[19] Interview, Frantz with Shivers, Austin, Texas.

Senate when they were not in the majority. This was, I know, not easy for him to get to this point because I know he went through a long, tortuous struggle . . ., but this was a significant vote. It meant a lot to labor. He was able to bring them all together. He had Paul Douglas and Harry Byrd sitting there waiting for the vote when the roll call started." Not in their offices waiting for the quorum call, not in the dining room, not in the cloakrooms, not somewhere in the chamber, but sitting there waiting to vote unanimously against the Republican majority. As Johnson told Birkhead, "If we have our forty-seven members well organized, this is a Democratic Senate."[20]

Again Johnson seemed to knuckle under to Texas conservative thinking when he led the fight to reject the nomination of Leland Olds as head of the Federal Power Commission in 1949. While the Olds incident is minor and not likely to be noted in any textbooks about the period, Olds was a darling of the liberals in the nation, and his rebuff by Johnson stung them more deeply than more nearly fundamental issues would have. As a member of the Federal Power Commission Olds had offended the private power companies by his advocacy of strong regulation. When President Truman reappointed Olds to the commission the private power companies reacted. So did Johnson.

It was a pre–Joe McCarthy campaign, . . . really vicious [Joseph L. Rauh, Jr., recalls]. The power and oil and gas companies were spending a lot of money; it's a sad fact, but [Abe] Fortas' firm was in on this thing with Johnson, and they really went after him. They quoted stuff [Olds] said twenty-five years earlier, which was pretty terrible stuff. . . . I'm not defending the crap he said . . ., but that's a different story than after he'd become a leading figure in the power regulations. . . . So there was a real confrontation between the liberals and Johnson. . . .

Paul Douglas . . . was . . . the floor leader for Leland Olds. He feels as I do [observed Rauh]—that was one of the dirtiest pieces of work ever done. And of course it killed Olds. I don't know how many years he lived after that, but he never really recovered himself.

---

[20] Interview, Baker with Birkhead, Washington, D.C.

Asked why Johnson took such a vindictive stand against the fore-most public-power advocate in the United States, Rauh admits to being puzzled.

> But all one has to do is to look at the *Congressional Record* [he noted]. Johnson read into the *Record* some of the most ancient stuff that Olds had said. And, as I said, it wasn't very pretty stuff, but a lot of things that were said in the Depression, a lot of things . . . that the people wouldn't want to say. God knows, I'll challenge anybody that . . . repeated everything he has ever said, because in a long and full life you say some pretty stupid things. I'm not saying that Olds didn't. I'm saying the using of that in the McCarthy way in which they used it to end the career of the number one public power advocate in America was a shocking thing, and it must be on Johnson's conscience.

Rauh felt that the Texas private power interests got to Johnson and that his stand against Olds did not represent a philosophical difference between the two men so much as a political necessity on Johnson's part. That makes Johnson's performance even less acceptable. Rauh cites the Johnson of the National Youth Administration and the Johnson of the early 1940s, adding that "Whatever anyone else says about Johnson, there's a certain Populism in Johnson's makeup that I would think would have [supported] public power . . . for the people. I mean, I can't believe that Johnson wouldn't ordinarily have the same exact reaction that all the rest of us would have, which would be [that] there's something good about public power."[21]

Johnson's role reminds one of some advice that Johnson received from one of his early Texas advisers. He was going to have to make up his mind, the man said, "whether . . . to be a Congressman or a gentleman."[22] In the Olds instance Johnson chose the role of politician.

Johnson's procedure in taming Senator Joseph Raymond McCarthy likewise remains questionable. His detractors—liberals mostly—damn him for his tardiness in putting down the Wisconsin senator. He dallied and delayed, they claim, while all about him good

---

[21] Interview, McComb with Rauh, Washington, D.C.
[22] Interview, McComb with Claude C. Wilde, Sr., Austin, Texas.

men were being blasted out of useful service because they had either dared to confront or had inadvertently blundered into McCarthy's headlong rush for headlines and revenge. In short, say the liberals, Johnson toyed with the nation's soul and intellectual safety while McCarthy single-handedly destroyed the validity of the Fifth Amendment and scared many Americans out of their historic right to read and write as they chose.

Joseph Rauh would disagree in part:

> I think maybe Johnson and Eisenhower were about the same on McCarthy, frightened by his bullying tactics. Bullies were always scared of other bullies, and I think that's what you had there.
>
> But we didn't get the slightest bit of help in the fight against McCarthy from Johnson, and to a degree we got hurt because he was always counseling, "Don't attack him, leave him alone," etc. That just isn't the way a democracy can work. It was a lot harder to call Johnson a communist for standing up to McCarthy, but Johnson wouldn't stand up to McCarthy.

Rauh unconsciously reveals the liberal's penchant for excusing John F. Kennedy while damning Johnson for similar behavior. He says:

> . . . of course when they finally put the censure thing through late in '54, the guy [McCarthy] was a drunken discredited bum. . . . And of course every Democrat voted that way except for John Kennedy, who was in the hospital and who had special political problems including the fact that his father was one of McCarthy's real backers, so I never got too angry about the Kennedy thing.
>
> I thought Johnson's position was really more despicable because there was no reason why he couldn't have helped us. In the end it came out all right, and I think the inoculation has been good for the country. I think we have less McCarthyism today because of McCarthy than we might otherwise have.

Rauh sums up: "Johnson was from, say, in the 50s a conservative Texan."[23] Like the advertisement for Budweiser, when you say *that*— that Johnson was a conservative Texan—you've said it all!

---

[23] Interview, McComb with Rauh, Washington, D.C.

On the other hand, Johnson has his claque of admirers who argue as vehemently and as convincingly that the Senate majority leader handled McCarthy the only way he could be handled—by letting the conscienceless senator extend his power until he became ensnarled in his own deviousness and then striking quickly and tellingly to destroy his influence once and for all. No question remained as to the sentiments of many of Johnson's Texas constituency. In the Texas view McCarthy was against communism, and any person against communism is all right, even if he is as deadly as Adolf Hitler.

Now, Rauh didn't particularly admire Johnson, though he worked with him periodically. To balance the account, let's look at one of Johnson's most perfervid though realistic admirers—Thomas Gardiner Corcoran—Tommy the Cork—the Franklin D. Roosevelt Whiz Kid who grew into a Washington elder statesman, though still hyperadrenalized. Despite his unabashed advocacy of Johnson, Corcoran sounds as vehement as Rauh on the Olds fight.

"I think he is ashamed of . . . [it] now," Corcoran told me in 1969. "I told him to his face one day. . ., that I thought it was the rottenest thing he'd ever done and that he could take it or . . . leave it. . . . I realize . . . what a crucifiable position Mr. Johnson was in between the troglodytic state of mind in . . . Texas related to oil and gas, and the needs of a nation as a whole." Summarizing, Corcoran observed, "The Interstate and Foreign Commerce Committee . . . did as dirty a job of trying to crucify this guy a la McCarthy as I have ever heard. . . . Now that's the only row I ever had with Lyndon."[24]

During the McCarthy days Johnson walked a political tightrope. Whether it was necessary can be debated but with no assured answers. During the senator from Wisconsin's period William Smith White went to Johnson to say, "You really must do something about this damned fellow." Johnson replied as follows:

---

[24] Interview, Frantz with Corcoran, Washington, D.C.

Bill, that's a good point, but let me explain something to you. In the present atmosphere, if I commit the Democratic party to the destruction of McCarthy [destruction probably meaning censure here], first of all we will lose and he will win in the present atmosphere of the Senate. He'll be more powerful than ever. At this juncture I'm not about to commit the Democratic party to a high school debate on the subject. Resolved That Communism is good for the United States, with my party taking the affirmative.

Johnson felt, according to White, that McCarthy was in a position to bring the "whole Senate to its knees."

"Now later on," continues White, "Johnson did indeed go after him and got him—got him in the sense that he brought about the creation of the select committee that investigated and censured McCarthy. But he waited until the atmosphere was right because he was afraid."

Not that Johnson was afraid of McCarthy as an opponent but only because of the lasting mischief he could deal the Democratic party, White believes. "McCarthy never would have dared take him on directly," he avers, "any more than, let's say, he would have Taft. But this was an illustration. . . . —I think an important one—of the profound common sense of Johnson to national issues."

White notes, incidentally, that the McCarthy issue represented the only time he ever volunteered any advice to Johnson.[25] Smart man!

In fact, according to George Edward Reedy, Johnson's former press secretary:

Johnson even developed techniques for using McCarthy. I can recall one day when we had a terribly close vote on the Social Security issue and every single vote counted. Boy, that was a rough one! Because the whole White House staff was up on the Senate floor, and we'd get a vote and lose two, and then we'd get a couple and lose one. They had "Slick" Persons up there and . . . a whole crew lobbying at one point.

Johnson looked at McCarthy, and he walked over to him, and he said, "Joe, would you really like to screw Eisenhower, and screw him good?" And of course Joe was real mad at the President at that point. By God, that was

[25] Interview, Baker with White, Washington, D.C.

one of the two or three votes, maybe even the vote . . . that put the Democratic position over.[26]

Harry Cummings McPherson confirms White's view of Johnson's caution where professional patriots were concerned—not on screwing Eisenhower. "He never had anything but contempt for McCarthyism, for hollering after Communists and all that," says McPherson, who served five years in the Senate with the majority leader.

He knew too God-damned many of them for one thing back in the 1930s. . . . And he has what Sidney Zion of the New York Times has said is probably the most acute sense of civil liberties of any modern President. But from a purely political point of view, he didn't want to go back to the days when Truman and the Truman Administration were under attack by Joe McCarthy, and the Democratic Party looked pro-Communist or looked as if it was soft on Communism.

The Johnson approach was to be tough on Communism, at home and abroad, and then to be able to get your liberal program through. He thought the odium attached to being soft on Communism would kill any possibility for progressive legislation, . . . from a hardheaded point of view he was right. [27]

McPherson watched Johnson through a similar fight on the loyalty oath that again placed the majority leader at odds with the liberals in his party. The script reads like a cloning of the McCarthy problem.

Jack Kennedy had authored a bill [recalls McPherson] that would have repeated the loyalty oath requirement in the National Defense Education Act. This had been the subject of great controversy and bitterness in the colleges. A lot of college presidents, on the motion of their faculties, had said, "If the loyalty oath is retained, we won't accept any assistance from the NDEA." The bill was reported out by the labor committee, of which Kennedy was a member—It was heavily stacked with liberals—so it got out. And for several weeks, I kept nudging him to take the bill up. And one day he turned to me and said, "I am not going to get the Democratic Party into a national debate: Resolved, That the Communist Party is good for

---

[26] Interview, Frantz with Reedy, Washington, D.C. Wilton B. Persons was deputy assistant to Eisenhower.

[27] Interview, McComb with McPherson, Washington, D.C.; used with permission.

the United States with the Democratic Party taking the affirmative."

He came finally, I think, to support that repeal [continues Mc-Pherson]. He didn't like the loyalty oath; it was a Karl Mundt operation and he had a sublime contempt for that frame of mind.[28]

Although many people believe that Johnson's successive civil rights bills as Senate majority leader and as President possibly represent President Johnson's most significant contribution to the progress of this nation, as well as his greatest shift in political position from a Texan with southern prejudices to a national force with liberal outlook, not too much need be said here about Johnson's work on civil rights. Monroe Lee Billington has already chronicled this change in a thoroughly researched and equally convincing article,[29] so that about all that can be added is window dressing.

No question exists that Johnson did shift somewhat as he changed constituencies. When he represented the reasonably moderate Tenth District of Texas he could probably be classified as moderate on civil rights, though the issue was not as sharply drawn in his congressional days.

But as senator from Texas Johnson pulled in his liberal horns to reveal a less attractive side. He supported the foes of antilynching bills, and he likewise supported the poll tax—the same poll tax which he later helped shuck from the codes of several southern states. But then, as a garden-variety senator, he represented all of Texas, which faces life from a basically conservative stance.

As he wrote one of his intermittent employees back in Texas ". . . if 'States' Rights' is to be a valid and responsible belief which progressive men can defend, then opportunities such as this should be passed by or ignored." Further, he cautioned, "social progress [should be] measured in terms of what is done for the mind, the body, and communication interlocking diverse areas and communities. The

---

[28] Ibid.

[29] Billington, "Lyndon B. Johnson and Blacks: The Early Years," *Journal of New History*, LXII (January 1977), 26–42.

Negro and Latin-American in Texas profits from many things other than the legislation affecting his status of well-being directly. What applies in Texas also applies nationally, although many lose sight of this."[30]

When he became Senate majority leader after his reelection in 1954, Johnson could feel secure that he had the power to continue as senator from Texas, for he had assumed a mantle of power—and Texans respect power, regardless of its political source or stance. He could neutralize the ultraconservatives, who handle the money in Texas and therefore underwrite or withhold from aspiring candidates, simply because Johnson was now who he was. Consequently, he could again become progressive, perhaps even liberal.[31] And down the road as President, he represented all of the United States, with a few disgruntled exceptions, and he had the political intuition to realize that the death of John F. Kennedy would make the nation more receptive and more lenient toward social advances for the less fortunate.

And so he struck, sometimes in too much haste but always with an impatience that was infectious and compelling. Whether his Great Society will be deemed a social and political success by historians awaits the judgment of future generations, but we can look about us now and see already that certain fundamental advances have been made that evidently will endure.

On this plane Johnson was consistent through the years, apparently biding his time until he could strike a blow here and there—"keep his options open," as he liked to say. William Homer Thornberry, who succeeded Johnson as congressman when the latter moved up to

---

[30] Johnson to Paul Bolton, July 21, 1949 (copy), LBJL; listed under LBJ, Names, Bolton, Paul, Box 12.

[31] Carl Alberts believes that Johnson's increased liberality as majority leader resulted from Johnson's brush with death during his heart attack in the middle 1950s. "After that," says the former Speaker of the House, ". . . [Johnson] began moving ahead, not as fast as the liberals wanted him to, but he began moving ahead with the national issues then. That was the making of the President back then." Interview, McComb with Albert, Washington, D.C.

senator in 1948, tells about being taken to New York to see the sights by the new senator. On one of New York's buses, crowded as often, an elderly Negro woman boarded to find no seats. Johnson arose to give her his seat, an act of courtesy generally unknown to Manhattanites regardless of race, color, sex, or ethnic origin. After they left the bus Thornberry complimented Johnson for his consideration of the black woman.

"I never see any woman standing," said Johnson, "black or white, that I don't think of my own mother and hope that if she is ever forced to stand on a bus, some man will show her the same courtesy."[32] To Johnson equal rights was a personal thing, not a piece of legislation.

Clarence M. Mitchell, Jr., who lobbied for the National Association for the Advancement of Colored People, came to support this view. At first suspicious and even put off by Johnson's way of working, Mitchell, who admits to the fact that in their early association Johnson would often indulge in plain talk that would cause the lobbyist's "hackles to rise," also admits that Johnson "did a good job teaching" him. "He was of great help to us [Negroes]," says Mitchell. "And that is, he said again and again that people should have the right to vote. This bill had in it a provision protecting the right to vote, so this made him for it as a matter of principle. And I found then as well as now, that if he was for something as a matter of principle, his ingenuity would take over and the seemingly impossible could be made possible."[33]

Johnson's concern for ethnic minorities often expressed itself in little things that men of high principle but less humanity might pass by. When an undertaker in a small Texas city refused to handle the remains of a dead soldier of Latin American descent, Johnson arranged to have the soldier's body shipped to Arlington Cemetery

---

[32] Private conversation, Frantz with Thornberry, Stonewall, Texas.
[33] Interview, Baker with Mitchell, Washington, D.C.

across the river from Washington, D.C., and to have the lad's family brought to Washington to meet President Truman. When Henry B. Gonzalez first ran for Congress from Texas, Johnson took time from being Vice-President to spend a day on the back of a sound truck touring most of the shopping centers of San Antonio, telling that city's Mexican Americans "what opportunities they had to elect their first Latin American from Texas to Congress.[34] Johnson had no stake in the election: San Antonio was not in his district; Gonzalez was not a particularly close friend; the Vice-President simply thought that the time had come for Texas to start recognizing a segment of its multi-ethnic population by sending a Mexican-American delegate to Washington.

And when Johnson purchased "The Elms," the home in which he lived as Vice-President, he and Mrs. Johnson filed an affidavit asserting that they intended to pay no attention to a covenant which came with the land which forbade its sale to Negroes. When they sold "The Elms" Mrs. Johnson told Sheldon Stanley Cohen to show the house to whoever was interested, regardless of color or ethnic origin. The house was to go to whoever agreed to the price, and in Cohen's words, no prospect was turned away—black, brown, yellow, Jew; he could even show it to "diplomats."[35]

Johnson's lack of self-consciousness represents another facet of this ability to place himself alongside ordinary people instead of on some higher plane as President. Sol Myron Linowitz, who is not exactly ordinary, remembers being flown to the LBJ Ranch, arriving at midnight to be met by an obvious farmhand, wearing stocking cap and driving a station wagon. Only after he was in the car did Linowitz realize that his "hand" was the President of the United States.[36] And the first time J. Roy White, a local architect hired to do some re-

34 Interview, Frantz with Charles Jahleal Boatner, Washington, D.C.
35 Interview, McComb with Cohen, Washington, D.C.; used with permission.
36 Interview, Frantz with Linowitz, Washington, D.C.

modeling for the Johnson ranch property, met Johnson, the Senate majority leader, clad only in his jockey shorts, came up to where White and Mrs. Johnson were standing. "I believe he must have had slippers on or something, but he was in his jockey shorts and nothing else. I didn't know whether to laugh, run, cry, or what. . . . Or look. But . . . [Mrs. Johnson] was just as much at ease as if he was there without jockey shorts, with pants on."[37] And George Eastland Christian recalls being told by the President that he was balding and ought to hide his thin spots. Whereupon the President of one of the world's two most powerful nations, with Viet Nam and demonstrators crowding him from all sides, sat Christian down on the toilet seat and combed his hair like a fond mother for a half hour before being satisfied with his latest attempt at coifing.[38]

While women don't exactly represent a minority, they do constitute an identifiable group that has received less than its due from politics. Johnson, who leaned on his mother and his wife for considerable advice and direction, never had misgivings about the place of women in political life. At his very first cabinet meeting as President, he said that "The day is over when top jobs are reserved for men." And a few weeks later, after having appointed some fifty women to government posts, he told the Women's National Press Club: "I would like at this time to make a policy announcement. I am unabashedly in favor of women." He went on: "I am insisting that women play a larger role in this government's plans and programs. Women have a willingness of heart; moreover, they have an instinct for rightness that is as important to decision-making as numbers or logic."[39] That this wasn't simply political rhetoric is indicated by the enlarged role of women in his administration.

Johnson is also given credit for having reformed the system of

---

[37] Interview, Frantz with Roy White, Austin, Texas.

[38] Interview, Frantz with Christian, Austin, Texas.

[39] Interview, McComb with Richard Walker Bolling, Washington, D.C.; used with permission.

committee memberships in the Senate, a progressive move of which not all politicians approve even yet. But Richard Walker Bolling, Democrat from Missouri, called the reform "quite a remarkable rule . . . which we have never been able to achieve in the House . . . everybody gets a good committee regardless of how junior they are; and nobody gets to be chairman of two committees, regardless of how senior they are. Before Mr. Johnson, that was not the case; and these seniors would pile up good committee on good committee and they would take every . . . damned chairmanship they could lay their hands on."[40]

Back to the treatment of blacks, McPherson tells of being with Johnson in his vice-presidential days when Senator John Cornelius Stennis, whom Johnson admired enormously, came in to protest the projected acceleration of civil rights under President Kennedy. Johnson responded by telling of his long-time cook and her husband, who doubled as Johnson's driver, having taken his automobile from Washington back to Texas and of their being forced to buy their lunches at grocery stores on the edges of town and preparing them themselves, of having to sleep in the car most of the nights, and of having to take to the fields to relieve themselves. "These people are the employees of the Vice-President of the United States, John," Johnson had said. According to McPherson, as a completely defused Stennis left the office, the Vice President gave McPherson a big wink, as if to say, "We've got him!"[41]

As President Johnson told the students on a sentimental visit to an elementary school back in Cotulla in 1966, he had taught there when the school had no lunch facilities, no school buses, no playground equipment ("I took my first month's salary and invested in . . . [volleyballs and softball bats] for my children," he recalled), and he had worked as principal of five teachers, while teaching three

---

[40] Ibid.
[41] Interview, McComb with McPherson, Washington, D.C.; used with permission.

grades himself, doubling as playground supervisor, coaching the boys' baseball team, directing debate, acting as song leader (that should have been taped!), and between times serving as assistant janitor. Yet, "In that year," he said, "I think I learned far more than I taught. And the greatest lesson was this one: . . . . Our greatest resource is the skill, the vision, and the wisdom of our people."

Then he told how in Cotulla he had learned "the high price we pay for poverty and prejudice." "How long," he asked, "can we pay that price?" His answer was forthright: "no longer." He summarized thus: "Until the day comes when we can no longer hear the hum of the motor before daylight hauling the kids off in a truck to a beet patch or a cotton patch in the middle of the school year . . . I say we will not be satisfied with those conditions."[42]

Where are we then? Invariably, we return to the fact that as his time in service passed Johnson's liberality seemed to increase, a direction not followed by all politicians. We must also admit that Johnson was not above playing politics with issues, for after all he was—except on Viet Nam, which defied politics—a consummate politician who studied and practiced the art full time. He played to his constituencies tunes where he thought he had to, and like Barry Manilow he wrote the songs for those constituencies where he thought he could, and he made them sing along, whether they felt comfortable with the tune or not.

Most of all, I see Johnson as a symbol of that New South that is now a century or so old. (I don't know when we stop being New and become simply the South.) But in all the crybaby era from 1865 through the 1940s and with all the racial travail, much of it unnecessary, of the 1950s and 1960s, the South grew and retained a nucleus of decent people who didn't desert but instead stayed and toughed it

---

[42] *Public Papers of the Presidents: Lyndon B. Johnson . . . 1966* (2 vols., Washington, D.C., 1967), II, 1347–50; first two quotations on p. 1348, third on p. 1349, and fourth on p. 1350.

out, ashamed of and humiliated by the actions of their antediluvian confrères, outraged by being assigned red-neck designation simply because of an accident of geographical birth south of the Ohio River, and hooted at by national comedians and pundit-authors because they talked more slowly and more softly and sometimes even took time to be polite.

But underneath the visible meanness of the South and southerners rested a hard core of decency lodged in the hearts and activities of decent people who could find no forum for their liberality among their own people. A person's first duty is to survive, as did the blacks for more than three centuries in the South, and as did many companion whites for the past century, feeling forever closer to the Medgar Wiley and Charles Everses, the James Howard Merediths, the lads at the lunch counters in the Carolinas, and the black children at Central High School in Little Rock than they did to their white brethren, insulated behind the walls of their air-conditioned homes and the lushness of their manicured lawns, talking about how blood would flow in the streets if the blacks or the browns or the poor whites ever got their share of the American Dream.

And then came Lyndon Johnson, big and sometimes gauche, and sometimes assertive and contentious, but almost always a compassionate man toward people who seldom tasted compassion, and he turned around many southern negatives, gave the deprived people a better opportunity to improve themselves through education, and guaranteed them access to some of the rights originally guaranteed in 1776 and thereafter, and in the process partially accomplished the impossible. If he didn't exactly change people's hearts, he made them self-conscious about their prejudices, and he helped the South to join the United States, perhaps even to take charge again.

If the foregoing sounds like effusive praise, let me say merely that I am more pro-Johnson than when I began examining the evidence that has produced this paper. In short, I started out to watch Lyndon

B. Johnson turn 180 degrees as he progressed down the road toward national importance. Along the way I discovered that he was moving in a remarkably straight line, a generally progressive line, with now and then an aberration that might be inexcusable but no more damnable than the aberrations that most of the remainder of us sometimes perpetrate.

William S. White, who spent almost a professional lifetime covering Johnson, confirms this attitude. Says White: ". . . as we all get older, there are changes. In a political sense, in the philosophic sense, I have not seen any great changes [in Johnson]. I think at the end his political philosophy was basically what it was at the beginning. Mind you, when he was in the House and in the Senate, he was from Texas. His constituency was different, and he wasn't as liberal as he was later, but that was because he couldn't be. I don't think his mind was changed. I think circumstances changed."[43]

And so the metamorphosis promised in tonight's title did not occur after all, at least not in the political philosophy of Lyndon B. Johnson. Times changed. All of us changed with time, and Johnson changed along with us and the times. He simply had more opportunity to affect those changes, and with his acute political perception he often led and directed and challenged us as we leaped over a barrier that had stood in our way for either short periods or, as in the case of civil rights, for centuries.

As Johnson told a news conference in the summer of 1965, "I am particularly sensitive to the problems of the Negro and the problems of the city and the problems which the shift in population has caused, the problems of education. . . . I want to do my best to solve them in the limited time that I am allowed.

"I did not have that responsibility in the years past, and I did not feel it to the extent that I do today. . . . I am going to try to provide

---

[43] Interview, McComb with White, Washington, D.C.

all the leadership that I can, notwithstanding the fact that someone may point to a mistake or 100 mistakes that I made in my past."[44]

That he made mistakes is undeniable. That he corrected many of them is equally undeniable. But through it all, his line of procedure is as consistent as the investigator is likely to encounter for a person whose constituency enlarges from one employer to a district of several hundred thousand voters to a nation of two hundred million. If tonight I have pulled no curtain to reveal a changing person, it is because no revelations were there to be found. To declare otherwise would be to maneuver the evidence and strain the conclusion.

In short, the jury verdict must be, insofar as Lyndon Johnson's metamorphosis is concerned, CASE NOT PROVED.

---

[44] *Public Papers of the Presidents: Lyndon B. Johnson . . . 1966* (2 vols., Washington, D.C., 1966), II, 742.

DOCTORAL STUDENTS

T he University of Texas at Austin maintains no roster of doctoral students listed by professor. The following chronological list was compiled from partial information at the history department and the Texas State Historical Association.

Renfer, Rudolph A. "A History of Dallas Theological Seminary." 1959.

Peterson, Robert. "State Regulation of Railroads in Texas, 1936–1920." 1960.

Davis, Ronald L. "A History of Resident Opera in the American West." 1961.

Reagan, Hugh D. "The Presidential Campaign of 1928 in Alabama." 1961.

Stephens, A. Ray. "A History of the Taft Ranch and its Role in the Development of the South Texas Plains." 1962.

Ellis, L. Tuffly. "The Texas Cotton Compress Industry: A History." 1964.

Reese, James V. "The Worker in Texas, 1821–1876." 1964.

Malone, Bill C. "A History of Commercial Country Music in the United States, 1920–1964." 1965.

White, Raymond E. "Private Electric Utility Executives: Thoughts on Public Ownership, 1881–1960." 1965.

Schuler, Samuel A. "Significant Questions Relating to the History of Austin, Texas to 1900." 1966.

Armistead, Paul T. "Retired Military Leaders in American Business." 1967.

McComb, David G. "Houston, the Bayou City." 1968.

McCorkle, William L. "Nelson's Star and Kansas City, 1880–1898." 1968.

Charlton, Thomas L. "The Development of St. Louis as a Southwest Commercial Depot, 1870–1920." 1969.

Crouch, Thomas W. "The Making of a Soldier: The Career of Frederick Funston, 1865–1902." 1969.

Rathjen, Frederick W. "The Texas Panhandle Frontier." 1970.

Jager, Ronald B. "The Democracy's Demise: Grover Cleveland's Rejected Supreme Court Nominations." 1972.

Athearn, Frederick J. "Life and Society in Eighteenth Century New Mexico, 1692–1766." 1974.

Ragsdale, Kenneth B. "The History of the Chisos Mining Company: A Social and Economic Study of the Terlingua Quicksilver District." 1974.

Mayer, Arthur J. "San Antonio, Frontier Entrepot." 1976.

Tijerina, Andrew A. "Tejanos and Texas: The Native Mexicans of Texas, 1820–1850." 1977.

Tucker, Leah Brooke. "The Houston Business Community, 1945–1965." 1979.

BOOKS BY JOE B. FRANTZ

Gail Borden: Dairyman to a Nation. Norman: University of Oklahoma Press, 1951.

The American Cowboy: The Myth and the Reality. With Julian E. Choate. Norman: University of Oklahoma Press, 1955.

An Honest Preface. Editor. Boston: Houghton-Mifflin, 1959.

6,000 Miles of Fence: Life on the XIT Ranch of Texas. With Cordia Sloan Duke. Austin: University of Texas Press, 1961.

The Texans-Tejas Today. With Charles Beamer and Bertha Mae Cox. Austin: Graphic Ideas, 1962.

Readings in American History. With J. S. Ezell and Gilbert C. Fite. Boston: Houghton-Mifflin, 1964.

Turner, Bolton and Webb: Three Historians of the American Frontier. With Wilbur R. Jacobs and John W. Caughey. Seattle: University of Washington Press, 1965.

Limestone and Log: A Hill Country Sketchbook. With Roy White. Austin: Encino Press, 1968.

Houston: A Student's Guide to Localized History. With David G. McComb. New York: Columbia University Teachers Press, 1971.

Texas and Its History. With Robert K. Holz, Mildred P. Mayhill, and

Sam W. Newman. Dallas: Pepper Jones Martinez Inc., 1972.

The Driskill Hotel. Austin: Encino Press, 1973.

37 Years of Public Service: The Honorable Lyndon B. Johnson. Austin: Shoal Creek, 1974.

Texas: A Bicentennial History. New York: W. W. Norton, 1976.

Aspects of the American West: Three Essays. College Station: Texas A&M University Press, 1976.

The Forty-Acre Follies. Austin: Texas Monthly Press, 1983.

Texas: Estudio de Nuestro Estado. With James B. Kracht. Glenview, Ill.: Scott Foresman Social Studies, 1988. [A fourth-grade text].

Lure of the Land: Texas County Maps and the History of Settlement. With Mike Cox. College Station: Texas A&M University Press, 1988.

There are also about sixty articles, eighteen chapters in books, eighteen introductions to books, and unnumbered book reviews scattered in various magazines, journals, and newspapers.

NOTES

Prologue

1. "JBF Quotes," Betsy Chadderdon Frantz Papers (in possession of author).
2. "Comments" from the Will of Joe B. Frantz, ibid.
3. Interview with Betsy Chadderdon Frantz, July 31, 1998.
4. Janet Reed, Superintendent of Grounds, to Betsy Chadderdon Frantz, Dec. 29, 1993, Betsy Chadderdon Frantz Papers (in possession of author).
5. Loose program, Apr. 25, 1994, Box 23, Joe B. Frantz Papers (cited hereafter as JBF Papers; Center for American History, University of Texas at Austin); letter from Robert Wooster to David G. McComb, Nov. 30, 1999.
6. Audio tape, Joe B. Frantz Memorial Service, Nov. 20, 1993.

Beginnings

1. Letter to "Wilbur" from Joe B. Frantz, Sept. 9, 1982, Correspondence No. 2 File, Box 77, JBF Papers.
2. Letter to Wayne Gard from Joe B. Frantz, Apr. 16, 1964 (1st quotation), Personal AM 1964 File, Box 15, JBF Papers; interview with Colleen T. Kain, June 23, 1999 (2nd quotation).
3. Interview with Colleen T. Kain, June 23, 1999; Sheffield File (quotation), Box 51, JBF Papers.
4. Sheffield File, Box 51, JBF Papers.
5. Standard Certificate of Birth, Betsy Chadderdon Frantz Papers (in possession of author).
6. *Fort Worth Star Telegram*, Nov. 15, 1987.
7. Interviews with Helen Frantz, July 19, 1998; Lisa Frantz Dietz, June 26, 1999. The date of adoption is taken from a letter sent by JBF to the Bureau of Vital Statistics, February 8, 1981, asking for his birth certificate. Correspondence File, Box 28, JBF Papers.
8. Told to author by Joe B. Frantz, 1968.
9. Ruby File, Box 51, JBF Papers. A niece, Florence, who was about the age of Ray, also lived with the family for a time.
10. Letter to Nellie from Joe, May 9, 1985, Family File, Box 80, JBF Papers. His nickname "Little Joe" may have resulted also because he had an older cousin named Joe Paul.

11. Interview with James Cotten, June 26, 1998 (1st quotation); Joe B. Frantz, *Growing Up in Texas* (Austin: Encino Press, 1972), 57 (2nd quotation); Joe B. Frantz, "The Small Town: A Foreword," MS, p. 2, in Writing File, Box 15, JBF Papers. For background about the Church of the Brethren see Ethel Harshbarger Weddle, *Pleasant Hill* (Elgin, Ill.: Brethren Publishing House, 1956). Joe Harshbarger was Ezra Frantz's stepfather.

12. Ruby File, Box 51, JBF Papers.

13. Frantz, "The Small Town," 4, 5. Frantz, *Growing Up in Texas*, 48–52; letter to Helen Frantz from "Joe," Dec. 16, 1986, loose material, Box 17, JBF Papers (quotation); letter to Douglas Nichols from Joe B. Frantz, Jan. 31, 1985, Trips File, Box 8, JBF Papers. Josephine wrote an angry letter to Joe for his printed description of Mary Frantz, and disputed many points of his characterization of her. She wanted him to stop making comments about the family in speeches and writings. Letter from Josephine to "Dearest Joe," Sept. 13, 1978, Naval File, Box 52, JBF Papers.

14. *Weekly Herald* (Weatherford), Jan. 4, 1951.

15. Frantz, *Growing Up in Texas*, 51; *Houston Post*, Jan. 29, 1961 (quotations).

16. "A Christmas Collage," typescript, Box 23, JBF Papers; also in "A Christmas Collage," from *A Texas Christmas*, ed. John Edward Weems (Dallas: Pressworks, 1983), 86; Ruby File, Box 51, JBF Papers.

17. Interview with Jim Cotten, June 26, 1998; Health File, Box 4, JBF Papers (quotation).

18. Frantz, "A Christmas Collage," 86.

19. *Dallas News*, July 9, 1968.

20. Frantz, *Growing Up in Texas*, 54–55; audio tape, Joe B. Frantz Memorial Service, Nov. 20, 1993 (quotation).

21. Frantz, "The Small Town." There is a gentler version of this story in *Growing Up in Texas*, p. 56, in which Mrs. Frantz does not admonish her son, but agrees with his action in hugging Fred. The version presented here seems more realistic for the time and place.

22. Frantz, "The Small Town."

23. *Daily Texan* (UT-Austin), Feb. 13, 1953.

24. Interview with Lisa Frantz Dietz, June 26, 1999.

25. Letter to "K.F." from "JBF," n.d., K. Faber File, Box 4, JBF Papers.

26. Letter to Jolie and Scott from Joe, May 12, 1983, Correspondence File, Box 77, JBF Papers.

27. Letter to David from JBF, July 6, 1970, in JBF file of the author.

28. Letter to Joe Frantz from Paul J. Thompson, Sept. 13, 1938, 1952 General Correspondence File, Box 43, JBF Papers.

29. Joe B. Frantz, c. 1985, "Speech, Autobiographical" File, Box 33, JBF Papers.

30. Joe B. Frantz, "Eugene C. Barker as Teacher," MS, in Barker File, Box 51, JBF Papers.

31. Letter to W. D. Aeschbacher from Joe B. Frantz, Jan. 26, 1967, Correspondence File, Box 3P214, Texas State Historical Association Papers (cited hereafter as TSHA Papers; Center for American History, University of Texas at Austin).

32. Interview with Helen Frantz, July 19, 1998; interview with Colleen T. Kain, June 23, 1999.

33. Joe B. Frantz, "The Christian Right," MS, c. 1981, in Mss and Queries File, Box 18, JBF Papers.

34. Joe B. Frantz, "Speech Autobiographical," n.d., loose material, Box 33, JBF Papers; *Corpus Christi Caller-Times*, Feb. 7, 1993; discharge papers, U.S. Navy, loose material, Box 37, JBF Papers.

35. Letter from Robert Wooster to David G. McComb, Nov. 30, 1999; interview with Jim Cotten, June 26, 1998.

36. Joe B. Frantz, "A Christmas Collage," MS, in Drafts to be Read File, p. 9, Box 23, JBF Papers. In the published version edited by John Edward Weems, "A Christmas Collage," in *A Texas Christmas*, p. 88, the captain's voice is left out. The version in the draft seems more realistic for the time.

37. Letter to Joe B. Frantz from "Kir" (C. H. Stewart-Lockhart), Nov. 30, 1970, loose material, Box 7, JBF Papers.

38. Letter to Lt. Joe B. Frantz from W. P. Webb, Dec. 5, 1944, Webb File, Box 75, JBF Papers.

39. Discharge papers, U.S. Navy, loose material, Box 37, JBF Papers.

The Journey

1. Walter Rundell Jr., *Walter Prescott Webb* (Austin: Steck Vaughn, 1971), 4–5; Necah Stewart Furman, *Walter Prescott Webb* (Albuquerque: University of New Mexico Press, 1976), 82, 88, 110; Walter Prescott Webb, *An Honest Preface* (Westport, Conn.: Greenwood Press, 1959), "Introduction" by Joe B. Frantz, 16.

2. W. P. Webb, Webb File, Box 84, JBF Papers. The handwritten note is not signed by Webb, but it is in his handwriting.

3. University of Texas Press Release, Nov. 9, 1977; Frantz File, Box 34, JBF Papers (quotation).

4. Letters to Joe B. Frantz from Vincent P. Carosso, Feb. 3, Apr. 28, 1958, Project with Vincent File, Box 64, JBF Papers.

5. From 1963 to 1967 Frantz worked without success with a similar difficult widow in an attempt to produce a biography of Vaslav Nijinsky, the great ballet dancer. Nijinsky File, Box 40, JBF Papers.

6. Letter to Joe B. Frantz from Walter Prescott Webb, May 28, 1949, Business History File, Box 57, JBF Papers.

7. Letter to "Dr. Webb" from "Joe," July 20, 1949, Webb File, Box 70, JBF Papers; letter to Joe B. Frantz from W. P. Webb, July 23, 1949, ibid.

8. Joe B. Frantz, "The Mercantile House of McKinney & Williams, Underwriters of the Texas Revolution," *Bulletin of the Business Historical Society* (Mar., 1952), 3–20.

9. Letter to Joe B. Frantz from Milton R. Gutsch, Jan. 26, 1951, Financial Records File, 1950–1951, Box 4S145, University of Texas History Department Records (Center for American History, University of Texas at Austin).

10. Webb, *An Honest Preface*, 196. Frantz commented in 1979 that the University of Texas needed greater self-esteem. It would not hire its own good students in preference for eastern mediocrity. See Joe B. Frantz, "Academe in Texas," *Academe*, 65 (Apr., 1979), 173.

11. Thomas B. Brewer, "The 'Old Department' of History at the University of Texas, 1910–1951," *Southwestern Historical Quarterly*, 60 (Oct., 1966), 229–246; also, Webb, *An Honest Preface*, 18–19.

12. Letter to C. K. Chamberlain from Joe B. Frantz, Feb. 21, 1962, General Correspondence January–February 1962 File, Box 4S53, University of Texas History Department Records.

13. Brewer, "The 'Old Department,'" 237–238.

14. Webb, *An Honest Preface*, 27.

15. University of Texas News Release, Nov. 9, 1977, Frantz File, JBF Papers.

16. Webb, *An Honest Preface*, 54.

17. Letter to Joe B. Frantz from W. P. Webb, Nov. 16, 1948, Business History File, Box 57, JBF Papers.

18. Webb, *An Honest Preface*, 48.

19. Ibid., 33; also in John Haller, "A Most Generous Offer," in *Three Men in Texas*, ed. Ronnie Dugger (Austin: University of Texas Press, 1967), 95.

20. Webb, *An Honest Preface*, 33.

21. Letter to "Joe" from "WPW," July 22, 1955, Webb File, Box 50, JBF Papers. This quotation is also in *An Honest Preface*, pp. 30–31, but the spelling of "cabbin" is corrected, which misses the humor of the quotation.

22. MVHA File, Box 43, JBF Papers.

23. Letter to "Doctor Frantz" from Harry S Truman, Apr. 29, 1955, MVHA-1955 File, Box 43, JBF Papers; Joe B. Frantz, "The Documentary Editor," Draft Speeches, Box 23, ibid. (quotation).

24. Letter to Joe B. Frantz from Rodman Paul, Mar. 4, 1965, loose material, Box 1, JBF Papers. Paul's reference is to Joe B. Frantz, "Adios to a Free Man," *American West*, 2 (Winter, 1965), 34–38.

25. Webb, *An Honest Preface*, book in Box 26, JBF Papers.

26. Letter to Herbert Gambrell from Joe B. Frantz, Jan. 10, 1962, General Correspondence January–February 1962, Box 4S53, University of Texas History Department Records.

27. Joe B. Frantz, "Prettier Than Most of Us," Miscellaneous File, Box 36, JBF Papers; also, repeated in Joe B. Frantz, "Foreword" in Furman, *Webb*, xi. The document appears to be the basis for the "Foreword."

28. Joe B. Frantz, *The Forty-Acre Follies* (Austin: Texas Monthly Press, 1983), 185.

29. *Dallas Morning News*, Mar. 17, 1963.

30. Joe B. Frantz, "Remembering Walter Prescott Webb," *Southwestern Historical Quarterly*, 92 (July, 1988), 22–23; also Furman, *Webb*, 180.

31. Letter to "Joe" from W. P. Webb, July 29, 1956, Webb File, Box 50, JBF Papers.

32. Letter to Benjamin F. Wright from Walter Prescott Webb, Dec. 18, 1962, Benjamin F. Wright File, Box 23, JBF Papers; American Civilization by Interpreters folders, Box 29, ibid.; Clio's Children File, Box 62, ibid.; *Dallas News*, Apr. 5, 1964.

33. Letter to Robert F. Metzler from Joe B. Frantz, May 16, 1962, Personal Faculty File of JBF and Western History File, Box 4S81, University of Texas History Department Records.

34. Letter to Walter Rundell Jr. from Joe B. Frantz, Aug. 11, 1971, Webb File, Box 70, JBF Papers; letter to Walter Rundell Jr. from Chester Kielman, June 26, 1973, ibid.

35. In 1986 Frantz signed a contract with the Texas Christian University Press to write a biography of President Lyndon B. Johnson. In a "Statement of Projects" he mentioned that the LBJ project would go on into the summer of 1988, but that he was a

"surrogate son" of Webb and planned to write his biography. McWhorter File, JBF Papers.

36. Letter to Aaron Copland from Joe B. Frantz, Mar. 18, 1971, Planning and Preparation File, Box 50, JBF Papers.; also Furman, *Webb*, 183.

37. *New York Times*, Apr. 9, 1972.

38. Ibid.; also *Washington Evening Star*, Apr. 16, 1972.

39. *Dallas Morning News*, May 14, 1972. See the report of the conference by Lon Tinkle.

40. Letter from Robert Wooster to David G. McComb, Nov. 30, 1998. Fred Cotten was an early mentor of Frantz, and the father of Jim Cotten who became Frantz's longtime friend. Frantz contributed fifteen signed entries to the third volume of the *Handbook of Texas*, with long articles on literature and music.

41. See L. Tuffly Ellis Correspondence, Boxes 3P214–216, Texas State Historical Association Papers (Center for American History, University of Texas at Austin); interview with L. Tuffly Ellis, June 22, 1999.

42. Letter to "Joe" from L. Tuffly Ellis, Aug. 16, 1967, L. Tuffly Ellis Correspondence, Box 3P215, Texas State Historical Association Papers.

43. "Insider: Dr. Joe B. Frantz, CCSU Turnbull Professor," *Corpus Christi Magazine*, 6 (July, 1985), 10.

44. Evaluations File, Box 4, JBF Papers.

45. Loose material, Box 17, JBF Papers.

46. *Alcalde* (Mar., 1955), JBF Vertical File (Center for American History, University of Texas at Austin).

47. Interview with Ronald L. Davis, July 30, 1999; interview with L. Tuffly Ellis, June 22, 1999.

48. Letter to David G. McComb from Joe B. Frantz, Nov. 27, 1973 (in author's collection).

49. Letter to Dr. Ronnie Davis from Joe B. Frantz, Jan. 20, 1964, Job Maneuvering File, Box 43, JBF Papers; letter from Ronald L. Davis to Joe B. Frantz, Jan. 22, 1964, ibid.

50. Interview with L. Tuffly Ellis, June 22, 1999.

51. Letter to Ronald from Joe B. Frantz, July 2, 1962 (copy given to author from Davis).

52. Letter to "Joe" from Savoie, Sept. 16, 1954, Oklahoma Press File, Box 43, JBF Papers (quotation); letter to "Dr. Choate" from Savoie Lottinville, Sept. 17, 1954, ibid.; letter to "Dr. Frantz" from Julian Choate, Oct. 20, 1954, ibid.; letter to "Savoie" from Joe B. Frantz, Mar. 29, 1955, ibid.; letter to "Dr. Frantz" from J. E. Choate Jr., May 30, 1955, ibid.; letter to Joe B. Frantz from Savoie Lottinville, Aug. 23, 1955, ibid.

53. Joe B. Frantz and Julian Ernest Choate Jr., *The American Cowboy: The Myth and the Reality* (Norman: University of Oklahoma Press, 1955), 24. At the end of the television series taken from *Lonesome Dove*, Larry McMurtry's cowboy saga, the Frantz and Choate book was mentioned as a reference for further reading.

54. Frantz and Choate, *The American Cowboy*, 63.

55. *Austin American Statesman*, Nov. 6, 1955.

56. *Time Magazine*, 66 (Nov. 14, 1955).

57. *Daily Texan* (UT-Austin), Mar. 3, 1958; letter to Dr. Julian E. Choate Jr. from Joe

B. Frantz, Nov. 23, 1955, Cowboys-Choate-OU File , Box 35, JBF Papers.

58. Letter to "Joe" from Savoie Lottinville, Nov. 22, 1955, Cowboy Letters File, Box 35, JBF Papers.

59. Letter to Joe B. Frantz from Frank Wardlaw, Dec. 31, 1957, Feb. 10, 1958, Classified Correspondence American Cowboy File, Box 4S54, University of Texas Department of History Records; *Austin American Statesman*, Feb. 11, 1962 (quotation); Cordia Sloan Duke and Joe B. Frantz, *6,000 Miles of Fence: Life on the XIT Ranch of Texas* (Austin: University of Texas Press, 1961), preface, ix–xii.

60. *Dallas News*, Aug. 6, 1961.

61. W. Eugene Hollon, "Foreword," in Joe B. Frantz, *Aspects of the American West* (College Station: Texas A&M University Press, 1976), 15–16. Hollon and Frantz knew each other well throughout their academic lives. They roomed together at conventions, wrote letters back and forth about politics, and cherished the opportunity to insult each other at public functions. A particular comment of welcome, perhaps best confined to an endnote, became a part of the folklore among western historians. Frantz explained this on a rare 1971 tape recording of his introduction of Hollon as the speaker at the fellows luncheon of the TSHA: "If there is an afterlife I hope to get there first because I don't want Gene Hollon to introduce me as I enter the hereafter. One reason is that I could head off his saying, as he says every time, 'Joe Frantz is like a fresh breeze blowing in from the outhouse.'" From a 1971 recording in possession of the author.

62. Joe B. Frantz, "Pineda," in *The Sand Dollar Book,* ed. Don Veach and Judy Walker Veach (Port Isabel, Tex.: Sand Dollar News Service, 1977), n.p.

63. Joe B. Frantz and David G. McComb, *Houston: A Students' Guide to Localized History* (New York: Teachers College Press, 1971).

64. Frantz and McComb, *Houston*, 5; MSS Houston File, Box 40, JBF Papers.

65. Joe B. Frantz, "Rural America: A Late Twentieth Century View," in *Kansas and the West*, ed. Forest R. Blackburn, et al. (Topeka: Kansas State Historical Society, 1976), 211, 213.

66. Joe B. Frantz, "On to San Jacinto," *Texas Highways*, 33 (Apr., 1986), 17. "Will You Come to the Bower I Have Shaded for You" was the popular tune played by the Texan army as it charged across the field at San Jacinto to win Texas independence from Mexico.

67. Joe B. Frantz, "Sam Houston: Texas Giant of Contradictions," *American West*, 17 (July–Aug., 1980), 65.

68. Joe B. Frantz, *Texas: A Bicentennial History* (New York: W. W. Norton & Co., 1976), 70.

69. Joe B. Frantz, "Introduction," to *Letters of Hard Times in Texas, 1840–1890,* comp. David Holman (Austin: Roger Beacham, 1974), 3.

70. Frantz, *Texas: A Bicentennial History*, 135.

71. Ibid., xiv.

72. Joe B. Frantz, "Lone Star State," in *Texas Reflections of Our Past* (Corpus Christi: Heritage Keepsakes, 1986), 6.

73. Joe B. Frantz, "Why Lyndon," *Western Historical Quarterly*, 11 (Jan., 1980), 14.

74. Joe B. Frantz, "The Lone Star Mystique," in *The Republic of Texas*, ed. Stephen B. Oates, (Palo Alto: American West, 1968), 9–10.

75. Joe B. Frantz, "The End of a Myth," Drafts File, Box 23, JBF Papers; also in *Southwestern Social Science Quarterly*, 45 (June, 1964), 1–15. Frantz considered this one of

his more important statements.

76. Frantz, *Aspects of the American West*, 44.

77. Joe B. Frantz, "Taming the West," in *Visiting Our Past: Americas Historylands* (Washington, D.C.: National Geographic Society, 1977), 321.

78. Joe B. Frantz, "Cowboy Philosophy, a Cold Spoor," in *The Frontier Re-examined*, ed. John Francis McDermott (Urbana: University of Illinois Press, 1967), 180.

79. Joe B. Frantz, speech to the Western Historical Association, Oct. 10, 1969. Western Historical Quarterly, 1 (July, 1970), 264.

80. Joe B. Frantz, "The Frontier Tradition: An Invitation to Violence," in *Violence in America: Historical and Comparative Perspectives*, ed. Hugh Davis Graham and Ted Robert Gurr (New York: Signet, 1969), 142.

81. Joe B. Frantz, *The Driskill Hotel* (Austin: Encino Press, 1973), 5.

82. Joe B. Frantz, "Business History," *Texas Business Review*, 31 (Apr., 1957), 8.

83. Joe B. Frantz, "Academe in Texas," 172.

84. Joe B. Frantz, "Foreword," in Carlton Stowers and Wilbur Evans, *Champions: University of Texas Track and Field* (Huntsville, Ala.: Strode Publishers, 1978), 5.

85. Joe B. Frantz, "Brief for the Prosecution," *Social Science Quarterly*, 56 (Sept., 1975), 300.

86. Frantz, *Forty-Acre Follies*, 162.

87. Letter to Pat Boone from Joe B. Frantz, Jan. 9, 1990, Nettie Lee Benson File, Box 33, JBF Papers.

88. Letter to Joseph David McComb from Joe B. Frantz, July 10, 1969 (letter in possession of author).

89. Joe B. Frantz, "The Trouble with Honor," Honor's Day Address at North Texas State University, Spring 1972, Drafts File, Box 23, JBF Papers.

90. Joe B. Frantz, book review, *Arizona and the West*, 25 (Spring, 1983), 63–64.

91. Joe B. Frantz, "History Looking Ahead: the Present and Future of the Texas State Historical Association," *Southwestern Historical Quarterly*, 70 (Jan., 1967), 370.

92. *Austin Statesman*, July 13, 1967 (Senate testimony in Washington, D.C.).

93. Joe B. Frantz, "Re-stocking History," speech to the Tri-State Humanities Conference, Rapid City, South Dakota, Sept. 24, 1977, Tri-State Humanities Conference File, Box 51, JBF Papers.

94. *Alcalde* (May 6, 1976), in Joe B. Frantz vertical file (Center for American History, University of Texas at Austin); Wardlaw Book File, Box 49, JBF Papers. JBF worked on a book of his speeches which was never published. He made notations, however, about various speeches that he had given and their significance.

95. Wardlaw Book File, Box 49, JBF Papers.

96. *Austin American Statesman*, Feb. 22, 1970.

97. Interview with Al Lowman, July 28, 1999.

98. Letter to Peck Westmoreland Jr. from Joe B. Frantz, May 5, 1967, Speeches File, Box 33, JBF Papers.

99. University of Texas News Release, Oct. 13, 1978, loose material, Box 7, JBF Papers.

100. Joe B. Frantz, "Prospecting in Western History," *West Texas Historical Association Year Book*, 40 (Oct., 1964), 3.

101. Michael L. Gillette (ed.), *Texas in Transition* (Austin: LBJ Library and LBJ School

of Public Affairs, 1986), 3.

102. *Washington Post*, Dec. 29, 1963 and *San Francisco Chronicle*, Dec. 29, 1963, Speeches File, Box 33, JBF Papers. The idea of western subsidy is now one of the major themes of the "New Western History," a revision of western historiography that began in the 1980s. Frantz, however, is not cited in the text or the bibliographies of *Writing Western History: Essays on Major Western Historians*, ed. Richard W. Etulain (Albuquerque: University of New Mexico Press, 1991), or in *The Oxford History of The American West*, ed. Clyde A. Milner II, Carol A. O'Connor, and Martha A. Sandweiss (New York: Oxford University Press, 1994).

103. Letter to Congressman Jake Pickle from Joe B. Frantz, Oct. 2, 1964, J. B. Frantz Biography File, Box 56, JBF Papers; National Park Service File, Box 12, ibid.

104. Joe B. Frantz, "Big Bend Speech," Big Bend File, Box 62, JBF Papers; the speech is also in Big Bend File, Box 40, JBF Papers. The "cowboy description" is probably Frantzian; there is no citation.

105. See White House File, Box 75, JBF Papers.

106. Letter to Arthur M. Schlesinger Jr. from Joe B. Frantz, July 22, 1960, General Correspondence File, Box 4S50, University of Texas History Department Records.

107. Letter to Arthur Schlesinger Jr. from Joe B. Frantz, May 29, 1961, Joe B. Frantz Personal Faculty File, Box 4S79, JBF Papers.

108. Letter to Mr. President from Joe, Nov. 23, 1966, Lyndon B. Johnson File, Box 49, JBF Papers.

109. Letter to President Johnson from Joe B. Frantz, Apr. 26, 1968, LBJ Preliminary File, Box 82, JBF Papers.

110. See miscellaneous letters, FG/704A, Lyndon B. Johnson Presidental Papers (cited hereafter as LBJ Papers; LBJ Library, Austin).

111. Memo from Joe Califano for the President, July 12, 1968, FE 12/Johnson, LB/2-3-1, LBJ Papers.

112. Report by Herman Kahn, ed. Wayne Grover, Oral History File, FE 12/Johnson, LB/2-4, LBJ Papers.

113. Memo to President Lyndon B. Johnson from Douglass Cater, May 28, 1968, Executive FE 12/Johnson, LB/2-4, LBJ Papers.

114. *Houston Post*, Oct. 16, 1975; Joe B. Frantz note, July 25, 1968, Conversation and Notes File, Box 75, JBF Papers.

115. *Houston Post*, Oct. 16, 1975; Joe B. Frantz note, July 25, 1968, Conversation and Notes File, Box 75, JBF Papers; Oral History File, FE 12/Johnson, LB/2-4, LBJ Papers.

116. *Daily Texan*, (UT-Austin), Apr. 24, 1978. In 1974 Frantz also conducted oral history interviews for the Zales Corporation with the idea of gathering business history information for libraries and writing a business history of the jewelry company. The book was not written. Zales File, Boxes 56 and 79, JBF Papers.

117. Joe B. Frantz, *Texas: A Bicentennial History*, xi.

118. Joe B. Frantz, "Soliloquy on State History," *Western Historical Quarterly*, 9 (July, 1978), 315–320.

119. Letter to "C. B." from Joe B. Frantz, Jan. 9, 1974, Si-So File, Box 5, JBF Papers.

120. *Daily Texan* (UT-Austin), Apr. 6, 1977, June 18, 1979.

121. Joe B. Frantz, "Eleven Years—a Summing Up," *Southwestern Historical Quarterly*,

81 (July, 1977), 44; interview with L. Tuffly Ellis, June 22, 1999.

122. *San Antonio Light*, Sept. 9, 1977.

Endgame

1. Scott Fleming, Memorial Service, Austin, Texas, Nov. 20, 1993.
2. Interview with Betsy Chadderdon Frantz, July 31, 1998.
3. Letter "To All My Creditors" from Joe B. Frantz, Aug. 22, 1988, loose material, Box 17, JBF Papers; interviews with both Lisa and Jolie Frantz confirm his ineptitude with bills.
4. Letters to Patty Hight from Joe B. Frantz, Oct. 24, 25, 1988, First Union Mortgage File, Box 4, JBF Papers.
5. Letter to editor of Marquis' *Who's Who* from Joe B. Frantz, n.d., Correspondence 1991 File, Box 4, JBF Papers.
6. Ralph Waldo Emerson, "The Tragic," *Dial* (Apr., 1844), quoted in Gorton Carruth and Eugene Ehrlich, *American Quotations* (New York: Wings Books, 1988), 524.
7. Letter to "Dearest Nellie" from Joe B. Frantz, May 26, 1980, Letters A–F File, Box 83, JBF Papers.
8. Letter to Joe B. Frantz from Terrell Webb, June 22, 1979, loose material, Box 71, JBF Papers; letter to Jolie and Lisa from "Dad," Aug. 2, 1979, Personal-Bills File, Box 31, ibid.
9. Manuscript copy of "Forty-Acre Follies," UT Manuscript File, Box 79, JBF Papers.
10. Letter to Joe B. Frantz from Lorene Rogers, May 28, 1979, Liberal Arts College File, 1978–1979, Box AR86-209, University of Texas President's Office Records (Center for American History, University of Texas at Austin).
11. Frantz, *Forty-Acres Follies*, 324.
12. There are still murky aspects about this incident which Frantz did not understand, but I have pieced together this account from the following: Frantz, *Forty-Acres Follies*, ix–xi, 323–324; *Daily Texan* (UT-Austin), June 18, 19, 26, Aug. 29, 1979; Don Massa, "Dr. Joe Frantz: UT's Past Makes His Present Tense," *Alcalde*, 73 (Nov.–Dec., 1984), 19–20; Joe B. Frantz, "My Assignment in Italy," Divorce File, Box 78, JBF Papers; letter to Jolie and Lisa from "Dad," Aug. 2, 1979, Personal-Bills File, Box 31, ibid.
13. Joe B. Frantz, "Reaganismo in Roma," *Texas Observer*, Dec. 12, 1980; Joe B. Frantz, "Prurience and the Pope," *Playboy*, 28 (June, 1981), 64.
14. Joe B. Frantz, "Diary to Italy, 1980–1981," loose material, Box 43, JBF Papers.
15. Letter to Frank Vandiver from Joe B. Frantz, Dec. 5, 1979, loose material, Box 1, JBF Papers.
16. Letter to Samuel Proctor from Joe B. Frantz, Jan. 18, 1981, Correspondence File, Box 28, JBF Papers; letter to Suzanne Comer from Joe B. Frantz, Dec. 18, 1980, ibid.; letter to Mary Hufford from Joe B. Frantz, Aug. 3, 1983, Correspondence File, Box 77, ibid. (quotation).
17. Letter to Joe B. Frantz from Mary Austin Berette, Dec. 2, 1976, BA-BI File, Box 70, JBF Papers; contract for YO Ranch book, Oct. 22, 1979, YO Ranch File, Box 75, JBF Papers.
18. Letter to Ronnie Dugger from Joe B. Frantz, Dec. 13, 1980, Correspondence File, Box 28, JBF Papers; also, letters in LBJ file of author.

19. Merle Miller, *Lyndon, An Oral Biography* (New York: Putnams, 1980); *New York Times*, Oct. 26, 1980.

20. Frantz, *Forty-Acre Follies*, x–xi, 337 (quotation); letter to Peter Flawn from Joe B. Frantz, Sept. 17, 1979, loose material, Box 58, JBF Papers. In the later audit of his expenses by the IRS Frantz was asked to obtain a letter of confirmation concerning his expenses from the president of the University of Texas. Frantz answered "no way" and threw out all of his travel claims. This compounded his tax difficulties. Letter to Carolyn Valentine from Joe B. Frantz, Jan. 12, 1988, University of Texas File, Box 83, ibid.

21. Letter to Fay and Eunice [Brown] from Joe B. Frantz, n.d., Correspondence File, Box 77, JBF Papers.

22. *Dallas Morning News*, Jan. 22, 1984.

23. Frantz, *Forty-Acre Follies*, xii–xiii.

24. Letter to Joe B. Frantz from David Weber, Aug. 29, 1979, Correspondence 1976–1979 File, Box 4, JBF Papers; letter to Joe B. Frantz from Martin Ridge, Apr. 13, 1981, Correspondence 1981 File, Box 4, ibid.; letter to Tom Johnson from Joe B. Frantz, Sept. 2, 1983, Correspondence File, Box 77, ibid.; application, J. J. Pickle File, Box 73, ibid.

25. Letter to Sue [Mrs Thomas N. Tengy] from Joe, June 27, 1985, Correspondence 1985 File, Box 4, JBF Papers; interview with Pat Carroll, June 18, 1999.

26. Interview with Pat Carroll, June 18, 1999.

27. Letter to "Hutch" from Joe, September 5, 1989, Correspondence 1989 File, Box 4, JBF Papers.

28. *Austin American-Statesman*, Mar. 14, 1986 (quotation); letter to Standish Meacham from Joe B. Frantz, Dec. 18, 1985, University of Texas File, Box 83, JBF Papers.

29. *Corpus Christi Caller-Times*, Sept. 7, 8, 1992.

30. Quincentenary—Corpus Christi File, Box 47, JBF Papers; letter to Joe B. Frantz from Tony Bonilla, Feb. 14, 1989, ibid., Box 65; *Corpus Christi Caller-Times*, Oct. 26, 1991, Aug. 27, 1992, Feb. 27, May 9, June 13, 1993. A review of the difficulties with Las Carabelas can be found in Mark Singer, "Texas Shipwreck," *The New Yorker*, 76 (Nov. 27, 2000), 78-84.

31. Letter to Tom and Jim from Joe, Aug. 17, 1988, Family File, Box 74, JBF Papers. Interestingly, and without explanation, there are two plastic cards indicating that Frantz was a sustaining member of the Republican National Committee for 1986 and 1987. These may have been a joke from a colleague—there is no other evidence to suggest Republican affiliation. Loose material, Box 8, JBF Papers.

32. *Corpus Christi Caller-Times*, June 7, 16 (quotation), 1987.

33. Interview with Jim and Dorothy McClellan, Aug. 3, 1998.

34. Interview with Pat Carroll, June 18, 1999.

35. A count of speeches and thank you letters amount to at least twelve talks in 1986. See Speeches File, Box 33, JBF Papers.

36. Ibid.

37. Letter to Judy Alter from Joe B. Frantz, Jan. 11, 1988, TCU Press File, Box 8, JBF Papers.

38. Letter to Joe B. Frantz from Mary Gordon Spence, May 29, 1985 [?],General Land Office File, Box 12, JBF Papers.

39. Letter to Mary Gordon [Spence] from Joe B. Frantz, June 6, 1988 [?], General Land Office File Box 12, JBF Papers.

40. Letter to Helen from Joe, Apr. 10, 1991, loose material, Box 41, JBF Papers.

41. Interview with Pat Carroll, June 18, 1999.

42. Interview with Jim and Dorothy McClellan, Aug. 3, 1998.

43. Interviews with Robert Wooster, and Alan Lessoff, Aug. 3, 1998.

44. "Quest for Peace," loose material, Box 37, JBF Papers.

45. Interview with Tom Kreneck, Aug. 3, 1998.

46. Note from Ross L. Purdy to Joe B. Frantz, June 28, 1989, CCSU #2 File, Box 65, JBF Papers.

47. Letter to Kristina from Joe, July 26, 1988, Kristina Faber File, Box 4, JBF Papers.; letter to Kristina from Joe, Oct. 2, 1985, ibid., Box 2.

48. Letter to Scott [Fleming] from Joe B. Frantz, Dec. 18, 1990, Family File, Box 74, JBF Papers; letter to Lisa [Dietz] from "Dad," Mar. 15, 1990, loose material, Box 39, ibid.

49. To Srs. John Patrick Carroll, Ross Purdy, et al., from Joe B. Frantz, n.d., JBF Health File, Box 4, JBF Papers.

50. Letter to Jolie and Lisa from Dad, Dec. 3–4, 1992, Frantz 1992–1993 File, Box 4, JBF Papers.

51. Letter to Gene [Hollon] from Joe, Jan. 11, 1993, loose material, Box 31, JBF Papers; letter to Helen from Joe, Aug. 13, 1992, Family File, Box 4, ibid.

52. Letter to Barry Cohen from Joe B. Frantz, Sept. 3, 1993, Correspondence 6/93, Box 30, JBF Papers.

53. Memo to David G. Mead from Joe B. Frantz, Dec. 7, 1992, loose material, Box 61, JBF Papers.

54. Commencement, TAMCC, Aug. 6, 1993, black notebook, Box 30, JBF Papers.

Epilogue

1. Quoted also in Joe B. Frantz, "An Appreciative Introduction," in Webb, *An Honest Preface,* 26.

2. Joe B. Frantz, "High, high, high, high—High Society," loose material, Box 22, JBF Papers.

3. Letter to Joe B. Frantz from David McComb, Aug. 27, 1977, black notebook, Box 36, JBF Papers.

4. Letter to Joe B. Frantz from George Woolfolk, Apr. 15, 1974, Woolfolk File, Box 84, JBF Papers.

5. Joe B. Frantz, "On Being Definitive," Drafts File, Box 23, JBF Papers; also published in *Southwest Review,* 44 (Winter, 1959), 72–74.

INDEX

ABOUT THE AUTHOR

David G. McComb, a former student of Joe B. Frantz and a professor of history at Colorado State University has written many books and articles about Texas, including *Galveston: A History and a Guide* which was recently published by the Texas State Historical Association. Following the completion of his dissertation in 1968 he joined the interview team formed by Frantz for the Lyndon B. Johnson Oral History Project. After a year with the project, part of which was spent with Frantz in Washington, D.C., McComb began a teaching career at Colorado State University in Fort Collins, Colorado. The Texas State Historical Association selected him as a Fellow in 1988.

COLOPHON

The typeface used for the text is Galliard, designed by Matthew Carter. The display face is Delphian.

One thousand copies printed at Edwards Bros., Inc., Lillington, N.C., on 55 lb. Glatfelter